PROGRESSIVES IN AMERICA 1900-2020

Liberals with Attitude!

DAVID WAGNER, PHD

Professor Emeritus
Sociology and Social Work
University of Southern Maine

Gotham Books
30 N Gould St.
Ste. 20820, Sheridan, WY 82801
https://gothambooksinc.com/
Phone: 1 (307) 464-7800

Published by Gotham Books (date published Jan 1, 2022)
First edition (2020)

ISBN: 978-1-956349-16-0 (sc)
ISBN: 978-1-956349-17-7 (e)

Library of Congress Control Number: 2021920257

CONTENTS

Notes on the Use of Progressive 7

One: Who and What Are Progressives? 9
    Introduction 9
    History of Progressives 15
    Analysis and Critique 20
    The Discredited Name *Progressive* 20
    The Elusive Progressive 23
    Not-So-Radical Radicals 27
    Progressives = Liberals with Attitude! 32
    What Would Be Radical? 33
    Book Organization.......................................35
    Table I Crib Sheet: Progressives, Liberals,
    Radicals on Issues; A Historical Charting
    (1900–2020)...37

Two: The Original Progressives: "The Radical
Movement Under Conservative Direction"..................47
    Context..49
    Muckrakers 51
    Radicals 53
    Progressives: Who They Were......................56

Progressives: Issue Consensus and Conflict..............59
From Progressives to the Progressive Party of 1924....70
Why All the Fuss? The Limited
Accomplishments of the Progressives......................74
Table II Progressive Party in National
Presidential Elections 79

Three: Progressives II: Fellow Travelers of Stalinism.......81
What's in a Name? 82
Context...85
The Popular Front: A Quick Deradicalization..........91
Why Did They Do It? Progressive Motivations 101
The Hitler-Stalin Pact 109
World War II 111
The Cold War and the Progressive Party of 1948 115
Takeaways: Continuity and Change 122

Four: Progressives III: The Rapid Decline of
Liberalism and Progressive as a New Name.................126
Liberalism's Collapse 127
Moving to the Right: The New Right and the
Centrist DLC..135
Why Progressive? The Popularity of Vagueness........137
Jesse Jackson: Not Radical but Liberal....................141
Nader Tries Progressivism outside the Two Parties ...153
More Powerful than Elections? 163

Five: Progressives IV: More Progressive than Thou 165
Clinton versus Obama: Will the Real
Progressive Please Stand Up? 167
The Cooling-Off of the Obama Love Affair............170
Sanders against Clinton: A Tale of Two Progressives ...175

The Trump Era: The Daily Battle............................184
The Battle of Progressives Rejoined: The
Election Season 188
Progressives = Liberals with Attitude! 195
Democrats as the Party of Finance and Technology.... 197
Summary 200

Six: The Left: Left Behind? 202
The Failed Left..203
Five Criticisms of the Left 207
How Progressivism Has Made Problems
Worse in Recent Decades 234
Things Can Change Quickly Sometimes...............238

References 241

index...257

Endnotes..279

NOTES ON THE USE OF PROGRESSIVE

I have listed the progressive movements as follows: the first the Progressive movement of the same era (1900-1917), the second the "progressives" of the Popular Front Period in the 1930s and 1940s, and thirdly the "progressives" of the past four decades and now. It is possible to argue that the 1924 Progressive Party was still another period, however, it is not generally accorded this status by historians, and it lasted less than one year.

Words like "progressive," "communist," "capitalist," and "socialist," for example, are used in different ways. I have used proper names for groups or individuals connected with a party or movement which is clearly labeled and identified as distinct political entities. Hence, the Progressives of the Progressive Era are capitalized, while those who were called this name in the 1930s and 1940s or those of the last decades are not capitalized (e.g. "progressives"). Similarly, those who were affiliated with the Communist Party or

Socialist Party are capitalized but those who have held these opinions but are not affiliated (or otherwise affiliated) are "communists" or "socialists," etc.

ONE

Who and What Are Progressives?

Introduction

The current political news in America is rife with references to progressives. Within the Democratic Party, at least three major candidates for president—Bernie Sanders, Elizabeth Warren, and (at least for a while) Kamala Harris—answer to the term *progressive*; but many other candidates, at least at times, use the term as a descriptor. Progressives have a large influence on the political debate, particularly in areas such as expanding health care, attacking climate change, and healing and remediating social justice issues. Only a few years ago, the term was far less used.

Some observers have waxed optimistically that now is the time for progressives. Mark Green's (a former Nader's Raider and an active New York Democratic office seeker for many decades) 2016 book *Bright, Infinite Future suggests* that

> "the core premise of *Bright, Infinite Future*
> is that there's a rising progressive majority
> and era in this country due to a combina-
> tion of demographic and social trends and
> a Republican lurch from the mainstream
> to the extreme." (Green 2016, p. 9)

Despite the irony of Green's book coming out shortly before Donald Trump's surprise 2016 election, a year later, Ruy Teixeira (a demographer and political scientist) declared in his book *The Optimistic Leftist: Why the 21ˢᵗ Century Will Be Better than You Think* goes even further:

> "Better days are coming [he says] … a
> new deal is just around the corner, bring-
> ing with what [he calls] an 'opportunity
> state.' Soon enough … progressives will
> take back power." (Jacobs, 2018)

Yet despite this new optimism, much writing is at such a high level of abstraction that it is impossible to see exactly what the fuss is about. Who exactly are the progressives?

What do they believe in? What is the history of their ideas? Are progressives simply liberals renamed, as some have suggested (McCormack 2018)? Are predictions about the future really simply promises of a Democratic Party victory? Or is there a leftist progressivism, as some political figures and their supporters declare? As a recent National Public Radio show noted, there is now a multiplicity of people claiming the name *progressive* (NPR 2018). Some of them use the term without adherence to any leftist view. Finally, even if elected, what would be the actual potential for serious change with, for example, Sanders or Warren as president?

One aim of this book is to answer these questions: Who are the progressives? Where did they come from? What is their history? What is their relationship, if any, to liberalism, to social democracy, to radicalism, or to other ideologies?

Further, as any number of critics point out, progressives do not make everyone happy and are opposed not only by conservatives but also by more radical leftists and by a surprising number of Democrats who believe liberal (or some other label) is far preferable as a description. To give some examples, conservative radio talk show host and writer Mark Levin has written an entire book on the tyranny of progressivism (Levin 2017) in which he uses documents from the first Progressive movement (1900–1917, see below) by the likes of Herbert Croly and Woodrow Wilson to condemn progressivism as a "statist" ideology summed up as follows (see p. 77):

> "Again, and again, the goal of progressives is to unmoor the individual and society from America's heritage with populist tirades, prodding, and indoctrination, the purpose of which is to build popular support for a muscular centralized government ruled by a self-aggrandizing intellectual elite."

But some liberals have been almost as caustic in their criticism. In an Op-Ed in the *New York Times,* Prof. Greg Weiner declared that

> "both etymologically and ideologically, the switch to 'progressive' carries historical freight that augers poorly for Democrats and for the nation's polarized politics." (Weiner 2018)

While Weiner sees the problem as being one of progressivism's rather absolutist nature-it is right and its enemies are wrong, whereas liberals can compromise with opponents—he also critiques more broadly *political correctness* as endemic to an ideology of progress. Another well-known liberal author Sean Wilentz distrusts progressives because

> "progressives are meanwhile 'emphatically anti-liberal'—because they are hostile to capitalism and 'deep down, harbor the hope that one day, perhaps through some catastrophic event, American capitalism will indeed be replaced by socialism'" (cited in McCormack 2018)

If conservatives and some liberals are critical of progressives, long-term radicals are likely opposed to the move en masse of many radicals (or former radicals) into the Democratic Party. As long-term leftist activist Stanley Aronowitz wrote more than twenty years ago,

> "the past thirty years have witnessed the incorporation of most of these (new social movements) and the older movements of the popular left into the framework of

liberal democracy. From deep skepticism according to which the law and the state were seen as instruments of class, gender, and racial power, the leading organizations of the popular left have made a more or less explicit alliance with the Democratic Party (1996, p. 105)"

If Aronowitz and others were critical of this move twenty years ago, now the criticism will be amplified and will be by some radicals such as the Green Party. It seems that thousands of former radicals are now actively campaigning for the Democratic Party.

The critical comments by various observers on all sides of the political spectrum bring me to my second objective: in addition to exploring the history of Progressive movements and activists, a more precise understanding of the politics of progressivism is in order. Because of the polarized political environment today, which appears simply as Trump and the Republicans on one side and the Democratic opposition on the other, political action and movements should be returned to its more complex situation than the current feuds. There is a deep continuity between today's progressivism and those of the past, and they are clearly separate not only from conservatives but also from the radical left.

Where liberalism and progressivism differ is more difficult to define, but a case can be made that there are some differences despite the fact that some liberals identify as both liberals and progressives or have moved from liberalism to progressivism. At least, progressives are militant liberals or as I say, liberals with attitude!

History of Progressives

Neither the term *progressive* nor its meaning sprouted from nowhere in the late twentieth and early twenty-first century. The current state of a progressive view and movement has come from two previous periods: one called the Progressive era beginning early in the twentieth century and a second one in the 1930s–1940s from left-of-center progressives allied with the Communist Party of the United States of America (CPUSA). As we shall see below, a variety of people and causes have vied since the 1970s to establish a third progressive movement. With some few exceptions, these political figures have been left of center, occupying a place that bridges the liberal wing of the Democratic Party with those to the left of it, such as socialists, pacifists, feminists, green and ecology activists, and others. I call this *bridging* as the term allows enough ambiguity to preserve the spirit of progressivism while presumably uniting those on the left with liberals in the Democratic Party. It reflects most directly the Popular Front period of the CPUSA, which some liberal and left writers look favorably on. [1]

The first Progressive movement and Progressive Party of 1912 led by former president Theodore Roosevelt have been well-defined by historians (see Hofstadter 1960, 1963; Kolko 1963; Nugent 2009; and Wiebe 1966). A middle class–led body of reformers (historian Richard Hofstadter refers to them as genteel) was not exactly a social movement but a loose association of those seeking reform. Progressive at the turn of the last century, history represented a left-to-centrist movement that included some US presidents, Theodore Roosevelt and Woodrow Wilson, as well as a large number of famous Americans such as Jane Addams, Louis Brandeis, Herbert Croly, Robert La Follette, Walter Lippman, Upton Sinclair, Ida Tarbell, and Lillian Wald. Perhaps its popularity is less in a common program (there was not one) but the fame and status of people identified with it (settlement house leaders, critical writers or muck-rakers who revealed horrible conditions, jurists, presidents, etc.). Less a grassroots movement than an elite one, it saw itself as a middle ground between the radicalism of groups like the Socialist Party of Eugene V. Debs and the radical union Industrial Workers of the World (IWW or Wobblies) on the one hand and laissez-faire capitalism on the other hand. At the time, Progressivism was marked by an emphasis on regulations such as antitrust laws, the Pure Food and Drug Act, and regulation of child labor. While there were some radicals such as writer Upton Sinclair on the fringe of the movement, it was a moderate to liberal movement generally.

In 1924, Robert La Follette, a popular senator from Wisconsin, ran as a Progressive against both the Republicans led by Calvin Coolidge and a very conservative Democratic candidate John W. Davis. The La Follette Progressivism was a short and unstable alliance that included labor unions, the Socialist Party, farmer and populist groups, and Progressive organizations left over from the earlier period. Had it succeeded, it may well have changed the history of American politics, but it quickly fell apart. And while La Follette gained about 16 percent of the vote, he carried only one state (Wisconsin, his own), and many believed his vote total was more reflective of respect for him than the movement (see MacKay 1947 and Unger 2000).

The 1930s and 1940s progressivism was centered around the American Communist Party and those liberals and others on the left who were willing to ally with them. With the exception of the 1939–1941 period (the Hitler-Stalin Pact led to a suspension of the Popular Front), it reemerged in the 1940s as American and Soviet troops fought together (sometimes called the Grand Alliance) and with the third Progressive Party of 1948 in which Henry Wallace ran as the candidate. The second progressive movement was more like today's in its emphasis on social justice, civil rights and civil liberties, and peace. Some authors speculate that the Communist Party chose the term *progressive* as a bid to reclaim the Americanism of radicalism in a respectable and Midwestern direction (see Howe and Coser 1962). The progressive alliance with the New Deal helped in some ways (making the party more popular for a while) but, more significantly, limited its ability to be anything but an echo of the Democratic Party. The party ceased to be radical, and in 1948, when the Wallace candidacy was widely viewed as being a CP front, Wallace received only 2.3 percent of the vote even with his vague program (see Chapter 3).

The second period of progressivism left a strong historical residue. First, the word *progressive* fell out of more mainstream usage for quite a while. Second, having been an activist in New York City in the late 1960s through 1980s, I met many older people who were in or had been around the Communist Party (CPUSA). Many continued to use the word *progressive* and, more importantly, like the 1930s–1940s party, tended to keep their identities quiet while claiming only to support progressive reforms. Third, like the transmission of the first Progressive to the second period, older people who remembered the Popular Front had a great deal of influence in the reemergence of the term *progressive*. One of main heritage of progressives is still the leftist support of the Democratic Party rather than independence.[2]

After a period in which the word fell somewhat out of the political vocabulary, it emerged in the late 1970s onward to replace *liberalism* for many. Certainly, by the 1980s, *progressive* emerged in the Democratic Party debate (for example, see Reston 1984 and Dionne 1988). The move of the Democratic Party to center in the 1990s created some confusion in the meaning of *progressive*, particularly with the founding of the Clintonian Progressive Policy Institute (see Ifill 1992). It is also not clear yet in the literature why exactly *progressive* was chosen as the label for disparate Democrats activists and their allies. Since then, a series of political events—notably the Iraq War, the Occupy Wall Street movement of 2011–12, the Bernie Sanders electoral effort in the Democratic Party in 2016, and the election of conservative president Donald Trump—have all strengthened a moderate left wing in the Democratic Party (see Edsall 2018) and presumably outside of it.

This book will present the historical continuities (and a few discontinuities) between the earlier Progressive movements and today's movement. I will also evaluate the chances of success of such movements against the many barriers of the American political system as well as political opinions that oppose at least some of their views.

Analysis and Critique

In addition to probing the history of progressivism as a movement and idea, I will also critique several features of progressivism as the term and orientation is used today. Key elements for discussion will, first of all, be the vagueness of its promise, which allows it a certain amount of protection from criticism, and second will be the strong contradictions that leftists, since the 1930s (and through today), face when entering the electoral arena as a field of action.

The Discredited Name *Progressive*

Back in the nineteenth century and earlier, Westerners following a wide variety of political views and theorists (and including theorists such as Comte, Hegel, and Marx) believed the world marched in a progressive course of history from worse to better. Westerners have an unbounded belief in progress despite many reasons to see humankind as in deep trouble. Progressive beliefs are deeply embedded in many religious, cultural, and philosophical beliefs. In contrast, the Far East and other parts of the world more often believe that history is cyclical—a belief that I think is much more accurate.

This quote from Andrew Jackson in an 1830 speech to Congress demonstrates the presumed uniformity of ideas when he addressed the removal of Native Americans in the Trail of Tears and also suggested the notion of a built industrial environment over a natural one:

> "What good man [*sic*] would prefer a country covered with forests and ranged by a few thousand savages to our extensive Republic, studded with cities, towns, and prosperous farms embellished with all the improvements which art can devise or industry execute, occupied by more than 12,000,000 happy people, and filled with all the blessings of liberty, civilization and religion." (National Park Service, speech of Jackson)

Amazingly, not just Jackson but almost all Western thinking since the Enlightenment, including the presumed enemies of the West such as the Russian Bolsheviks and other Marxists, have held similar views. They privileged industrial development and production and technology over the environment, over the indigenous people, and over a multitude of other cultural and philosophical interests.

In the aftermath of the 1960s, many social scientists and many activists who identified with the left, including later feminists and environmentalists, broke with the progressive faith and began to criticize the worldview that dominated the West for two hundred years. The development of industry and technology was not held as a positive good and came at the expense not only of indigenous people in America but also all over the world. It privileged the West's view of science and technology over non-Western views. It also endangered the environment and brought about the problematic state of the world's natural environment. Most people on the left believe this, yet still, some embrace a word so fraught with negativism. In fact, people in other countries, particularly Eastern ones, hold a very different view of history, generally supporting a more cyclic view of history and life. Why those who now support progressive candidates ignore the basic ideology of what they subscribe to is a deep puzzle to me.

The Elusive Progressive

A feature shared by most politicians and many activists who are progressive is the vagueness of their political actions and prescriptions. Of course, to some extent, all political ideologies are elastic and plastic; conservatives do not always act or even vote conservatively nor do liberals act liberally. Politicians and officials do compromise and adhere to what they see as the interest of the city, state, or nation. However, supposed progressives have been held to a wide variety of criticism not from opponents but by presumed supporters in almost every election and in almost every area of the country. One wonders how believers can support each election candidate who does not accomplish much of what their rhetoric implies.

To take just two examples from the nation's largest city and one of its largest states with one of the most progressive voting populations, neither former governor of New York Mario Cuomo nor current mayor of New York City, Bill de Blasio, can escape serious criticism from activists. In 1988, after six years of Cuomo's leadership, the *New York Times* correspondent Jeffrey Schmalz described the contradictions of his administration:

"The Mario Cuomo on the road who is the champion of the poor and the Mario Cuomo at home in New York (is very different), where a severe housing shortage has more than doubled the number of homeless people since he took office … What the observers, especially liberal Democrats, do suggest as Mr. Cuomo enters his sixth year in office is that he has not always practiced what he has preached. He criticized President Reagan, for example, for cutting taxes excessively, thereby limiting money available for the poor. Yet Mr. Cuomo signed into law last year the largest tax cut in New York State's history, later acknowledging that it was too big and would drain money that could have gone to social-welfare programs to offset Federal cutbacks." (Schmalz, 1988)

Thirty years later, the *New York Times* reporters noted that despite his social justice rhetoric, de Blasio had "disappointed some of his most loyal backers, who point to a range of issues, from criminal justice reform and homelessness to the protection of immigrants, where the mayor has fallen short of his promises" (Goodman and Neuman 2018). Perhaps even more telling than the criticism was his response that cited "efforts to improve police discipline, end solitary confinement for young inmates, and create neighborhood homeless shelters" as being progressive. Why should improving police discipline or building homeless shelters be considered progressive is not clear to me. Again, vagueness twists the notions of liberalism, progressivism, and other *isms* into a pretzel. Homeless people often do not support shelters that are inhumane, crowded, and dangerous. Police discipline sounds nice but not to those hurt by police officers.

As we shall see later in the book, the vagueness of the word combined with the lack of any strategy to secure *social justice* (whatever this equally vague term may mean) suggests conflict each election year for the Democrats. For examples, I will note the battles in 1988 between Michael Dukakis and his primary competitors, of Bill Clinton and his competitors in the 1990s, of Al Gore and John Kerry in the 2000s, of Barack Obama and Hillary Clinton in their 2008 showdown, and of course, of the 2016 battle between Hillary Clinton and Bernie Sanders.

The writer Edward Luce (2018, p. 47) puts his finger on the dramatic failure of all progressive leaders of the American cities:

"One of the ironies of the West's booming cities is how much lip service its more fortunate denizens pay to a progressive world view. We could hardly ask for a nicer elite. Yet the effects of how they spend their money are hardly progressive. For all the emphasis we place on multicultural cities, they epitomize our oligarchic reality. In the US the more liberal a city's politics, the higher the rate of 'inequality'."

In fact, few citizens who have visited New York City; Boston; Los Angeles; San Francisco; Seattle; Portland, Oregon; Chicago; Washington, DC; and other large American cities can dispute the presence of extreme deprivation often not far from the most luxurious of accommodations. While there's no doubt that mayors and officials will say they are limited by the federal government, they fail to answer why sixteen years of Democratic administrations (Clinton in 1993–2001 and Obama in 2009–2017) failed to change anything much or why the local or even state officials should be regarded as champions of social justice.

Not-So-Radical Radicals

The general strategy of progressives from the Popular Front period of the Communist Party (see chapter 3) to today consists of a naive attempt to support or infiltrate the Democratic Party, a top-down strategy as compared with grassroots organizing efforts made by many radicals in American history (see below). Using the vague rubric of peace or social justice or economic justice, these efforts sometimes bring brief success but at a considerable cost.

In the 1930s, after the endorsement of the Communist Party of the New Deal in 1936, leaders and activists were in a heady state, believing they had finally found a way to Americanize communism. Dorothy Healey's wonderful book (with Isserman in 1993) about her many decades in the CP as a party leader shows the enormous boom of party membership and spirit as they helped liberals and progressives be elected. Three examples of politicians in the Democratic Party whom Healey waxes on about were Gov. Culbert Olson of California, assemblyman Sam Yorty (later mayor of San Francisco), and Jack Tenney. Interestingly, within a few years, these CP-allied progressives turned on the party. Healey is almost matter-of-fact in retelling this:

"Jack Tenney also was considered the 'red assemblymen' a little ironic considering [his] subsequent career (leading the anti-communist Tenney Committee) ... and (Tenney and Yorty) ... both became red-baiters ... in a few years he (Yorty) was making a name for himself ... by becoming the scourge of the supposed Communist plot to take over the state relief agency." (Healey and Isserman 1993, p. 85)

And the party's friend Governor Olson? He, too, broke with the communists shortly after the Hitler-Stalin Pact was made public in 1939. And two years later, he demanded Healey's resignation from her position as a deputy commissioner of Labor of California. Her days of infiltrating the bureaucracy were over (see ibid., p. 86).

I will address the CP strategy more systematically in chapter 3, but what is amazing is the naivete of the party and its supporters in believing the Democratic Party would quietly make room for them. The only way an alliance was possible was a one-way alliance in which the CP supported the Democrats, but the vague program of this era (like today) meant that mouthing about economic and social justice and other issues led the radicals to believe they had something in common with the pro-capitalist party officials. Even more concerning was the top-down method the CP adopted in the mid-1930s and 1940s. Rather than organize people at the level of community and workplace and other arenas, the party became self-impressed with getting major figures in art, science, politics, and elsewhere to sign petitions and make speeches in support of communist fronts for peace, student activism, labor rights, and so forth. One of the reasons that few people stood up against the prosecution of Communists by the late 1940s (the McCarthy era) was their surreptitious and undemocratic tactics in taking over many organizations while not openly discussing or revealing their politics.

Although not identical, the recent moves by progressives and supposed socialists like Bernie Sanders to achieve the presidency and the popularity of recently elected congressperson Alexandria Ocasio-Cortez contain the similar elements of naivete, vagueness, and top-down beliefs. Sanders had a long career as a leftist, doing good organizing work in Vermont. Apparently, he became tired of his lack of fame and power and switched from an independent to caucusing with the Democratic Party in the 2000s. Although he essentially repudiated his entire career as an independent, he made a surprisingly strong run for president in 2016, albeit unsuccessfully, against Hillary Clinton.

But what has Sanders achieved exactly? Why after a century or more of fighting socialism would the Democratic Party embrace Sanders (or Ocasio-Cortez)? Opposition that helped Clinton win the nomination in 2016 seemed surprising to Sanders as opposition seemed to surprise AOC. And if they were to become more popular, on what basis? Both Sanders and AOC can respond to questions of what socialism is with only vague remarks, which make socialism sound like a form of liberalism. When asked valid questions about the history of socialism in the twentieth and twenty-first centuries, Sanders characteristically ducks these questions, not willing to talk about Cuba or China or Venezuela or the former Soviet Union. In 2016, Sanders implied Sweden was socialist, which is quite a surprise to its citizens and its enormous capitalist companies like IKEA, Volvo, and H&M, to name only a few. Perhaps, he and other progressives mean social welfare systems, but they have nothing to do with whether a country is capitalist or socialist.

In addition to naivete and vagueness, the progressives seem to use elections as a substitute for grassroots organizing. The idea seems to be that one puts oneself out there, runs for election, and magically gains support for many controversial policy changes. But this will not occur. Even some of the policy suggestions popular at times, like universal health care, recede when they are attacked by critics who talk about taxes and differential treatment of some people over others (for example, see Suderman 2019). More importantly, as has been clear for nine decades, the medical industry will not give up its power without a huge fight. Nowhere are people prepared to fight the big pharmaceutical industry, the huge insurance conglomerate, the hospitals, the physicians, and many related medical companies. The real issue is the profit in American health care, but the progressives do not confront this or prepare people (who generally have been taught to believe the medical industry is their friend). Even the highly unlikely election of Sanders as president (and AOC as vice president) would by no means ensure any major change in health care. Leaving aside opposition from their own party and Congress, popular opinion is too vague and mild to support a major struggle with the health-care industry. Though naive, I do not believe Sanders and AOC (or presidential candidate Elizabeth Warren) are so naive as to believe they will really achieve anything like this. Their real goal would probably be a variant of the mild Affordable Care Act, which was carefully tailored to the needs of the health-care industry and lobbyists (see Gibson and Singh 2012). Until we see people ready to demonstrate at the sites of medical centers and corporations, I do not believe great change will occur.

Progressives = Liberals with Attitude!

Despite some family fights as noted above, progressives ultimately are liberals, but of a special type. They certainly are not conservatives in a political sense, and Levin is correct that progressivism (in all three eras) is and was statist. It is certainly not related to libertarian ideologies, but its opposite. As I have noted (see below as well), they are not radicals at least as most social scientists or other scholars define it. They are not Marxists or anarchists or socialists although, at times, their rhetoric sounds radical.

It is the latter feature that seems to make modern progressivism unique. While originally, progressive was a label for a particular brand of reformer, after the 1930s and 1940s with the experience of many activists in the left (mostly the Communist Party), progressives absorbed an élan that saw themselves as a vanguard of consciousness and a keeper of a particular type of leftist reform, although never beyond reforms. The two caveats to note in seeing liberal as radical is that liberalism is a different animal at the few times in American history where a considerable number of people who join their camp do not think of themselves as part of the system. Something like this happened, for example, in 1972 with George McGovern as a presidential candidate, when a considerable number of campus activists and other new political activists joined his campaign or voted for him. Particularly since the election of Donald Trump, the conventional wisdom of voting for one of the two parties or being cast as a spoiler or worse (see Ralph Nader's treatment by media and the Democratic Party) has brought many once-radical people into at least a temporary alliance with liberals. Second, as time changes, the issues and emphasis change. Some older liberals are troubled by many aspects of millennial activist politics such as identity politics (to be discussed later), which privileges women and nonwhites, and a sort of arrogance about there being only one understanding of an issue (e.g., political correctness, which I also will discuss) prevailing. Of course, the left changes focus and so does progressivism; it is no longer an ideology about the issue of socialism but about the many issues that developed out of the New Left and other new social movements. This certainty and its prescriptiveness are definitely "liberalism with attitude!" that carries both strengths and weaknesses as well.

What Would Be Radical?

Although not the major focus of this book, it is appropriate to ask what movements and political efforts have worked in the past and how these efforts were more successful than progressive efforts.

Several movements that were successful include the Socialist Party's success in the 1900–1917 period, which, along with the famous Wobblies labor organizing (the Industrial Workers of the World), helped stimulate the Progressive movement by fighting well to its left; the actions of movements in the early 1930s, which helped create the crisis that led to the New Deal (for example, the Townsend movement, a grassroots efforts for pensions that helped enact the Social Security Act); the Unemployed Councils, a series of organizations and protests of the unemployed, which included Communists, Socialists, and followers of the Christian pacifist AJ Muste; and a large number of strikes that eventually led to the Wagner Act, ensuring collective bargaining. In the 1960s, groups like Students for a Democratic Society (SDS) and the Black Panther Party (BPP) avoided electoral politics but helped develop the anti–Vietnam War movement and a more radical pro-socialist movement. In more recent times, the Seattle protests in 1999 showed the ability of a coalition of groups to shut down a major meeting of the World Trade Organization (WTO).

Unfortunately, in recent years, lack of leadership and fear have paralyzed what could have been other successful movements. The initial outbreak of spontaneous demonstrations of the Occupy Wall Street movement in 2011 raised for millions of people the issues of income inequality and the domination of Wall Street and big business over American life. However, the demonstrators had no clear demands and no clear target to their organizing. Here and there, successful demonstrations were held (for example, against corporations). However, just as progressives are stuck trying to influence elections as Democratic Party members, more radical forces are paralyzed in taking no actions that would be highly controversial, lead to arrests and possible retaliation at workplaces, and alienate friends and family. Still, the way forward, in my view, cannot be dominated by fear and by listening to those on the liberal-progressive left.

Book Organization

The major part of this book (chapters 2–5) will review and assess the history of the loosely connected efforts of progressives: the first Progressive era, primarily of the first two decades of the twentieth century but continuing with the 1924 election; the progressives of the 1930s and 1940s and their efforts in the New Deal and Fair Deal era (roughly 1936–1948); and the beginnings in the late 1970s and 1980s continuing to today's groups of activists and political leaders who have also attached themselves to the progressive label.

In chapter 6, I will return to analysis to look at the current configuration of American politics and the conclusion that the new progressivism is old wine in new jugs. While using heated rhetoric at times, it reflects the continuation of a liberal attempt at reform. It is not any sort of radicalism or socialism but is merely heated liberalism. Like the Democratic victories in 1976, 1992, 1996, 2008, and 2012, even if they win, the results will not be very much changed.

However, the problems of the twenty-first century are not confined to progressives but have seriously confined the left to a marginal role not only in the United States but also in most of the world. The reasons for this are both some severe theoretical shortcomings and some problems of practice that distance people of whatever class, race and ethnicity, gender, or sexual orientation from the left. I do not have the room to discuss all the remedies to these problems, and it is far too soon to see if these problems are inevitable.

For those who are helped by crib sheets, I have attached to this chapter a table that helps introduce the book further. The table 1 (Crib Sheet: Progressives, Liberals, Radicals on Issues; A Historical Charting [1900–2020]) provides a short and generalized summary of where liberals and progressives stand on issues over time.

Table I
Crib Sheet: Progressives, Liberals, Radicals on Issues; A Historical Charting (1900–2020)

Capitalism, Socialism, and Reform

- Conservatives support capitalism.
- Progressive reformers have always supported the capitalist economic system though they seek to reform it in different ways. The leaders of the initial Progressive movement, the La Follette candidacy in 1924, and the leaders of liberal Democrats from Roosevelt on all condemned socialism by any name. The original Progressive movement hoped that the regulation of industry would curb the total dominance of business over both the worker and the consumer, and the Progressive Party in 1924 continued in this direction. Despite the fact that the CPUSA allied with the Roosevelt administration in the 1930s and during the war in the

1940s, FDR never had a kind word for socialism. Of course, liberals hoped the reforms of the 1930s onward—such as the Social Security Act, the National Labor Relations Act, public works programs, etc.—would alleviate some of capitalism's problems.

- Most groups termed *radical* oppose the capitalist system and believe only revolutionary change will produce socialism or another other kind of non-capitalist system.

Environmental Issues

For the most part, the environment was not a major issue until the 1970s although the original Progressives did champion conservation efforts.

- In the 1970s, some liberal political leaders and many activists from the 1960s and 1970s became involved. Certainly, many of these environmental activists identified as liberal or progressive.
- However, with time, new more radical organizations were formed generally with the dividing line being the more radical groups did not think capitalism and a safe and sustainable world were com-

patible. The recent concern with climate change has been affected to a great degree by the refusal of some political leaders of the right to accept that it is human-made rather than anything intrinsic to the issue, but this does not make it a radical issue.

• It is unfair to characterize conservatives as anti-environmentalists. But they are certainly suspicious of many environmental claims, and they worry about the ability of our system to sustain the costs of changes proposed by radicals and sometimes liberals.

Foreign Policy and War

This area has been a totally different vector from domestic policy, and the views in American history have sometimes quickly shifted. In World War I, Progressives and conservatives and liberals, for the most part, supported the war once Woodrow Wilson declared it. Robert La Follette was among the few major leaders who opposed it, and in the 1920s, a movement among progressives became anti-war. Those opposed going to war in the 1930s until Pearl Harbor included both progressives (or former Progressives) and conservatives whom Franklin Roosevelt condemned as isolationists.

- The Democratic liberal leadership and its allies became more pro-war as the 1940s came. During the long Cold War, it was very rare to find dissenters at all from the Cold War until the Vietnam War brought about a surprisingly successful protest movement. But despite the association of some liberals and progressives with the anti-war movement, most political leaders in the Democratic Party supported foreign interventions in the late twentieth century through today. Most of the, at least, seven wars we are in have been continued under both the Obama and Trump administrations.

- Only some radicals and socialists have been consistent in opposing wars in Iraq, Afghanistan, Yemen, Libya, Somalia, and elsewhere.

- Conservatives have become split on issues of war and foreign policy. The mainstream Republican Party, such as both Bushes, are for an active interventionist nation. However, some more populist conservatives are more isolationist, and they believe the USA should abandon at least some of its overseas ventures.

Immigration Issues

Here, there has been some changes. Generally, prior to recent years, conservatives, liberals, and radicals were supportive of limiting immigration. Since employing groups were mostly conservative and favored using immigrant labor, it can be suggested that they were more for immigration than, for example, the union movement, which saw immigration as detrimental to their wage rates.

- It is hard to pin down an exact date for the changes, but it appears that the large number of immigrants of Mexican/Latino and Asian-American descent, which now comprise a large percentage of the US population, has shifted liberal and progressive thinking to a position of support for all immigration. It appears, for the most part, to have also convinced labor leaders, although not necessarily their rank and file, to support immigration. Dependent on how this issue is framed, it can lead a majority of Americans to oppose unrestricted immigration or, in other words, to have a majority support relatively free immigration.
- Radicals seem to have adopted an open-border position.

- Conservatives are more associated with opposition to unrestricted immigration although some corporate leaders who are conservative may not agree.

Income, Egalitarianism, and Social Welfare

Along similar lines to the above, the progressive movements have not favored any sort of complete leveling of society.

- Both the original Progressive movement and its 1920s version sought some reforms but, for the most part, not in income or wages per se. The Great Depression and the need to intervene in the economy led the New Deal, for the first time in American society, to support a very conservative welfare state, including Social Security and unemployment insurance systems that were based on prior earnings and work experience. It rejected again and again any effort to provide social benefits to all who might be eligible. It also established a minimum wage that remained well below prevailing wages throughout the years. More attention among liberals may have come in the 1960s and 1970s when part of the civil rights movement, such as the welfare rights movement, began to protest the low benefits of welfare as well as racism and paternalism in the system. Some veterans of the '60s and some millennial progressives (and radicals) do support efforts to substantially raise wages (such as living wage campaigns or efforts to raise the minimums) and/or guaranteed income for all, particularly in light of all the massive technology changes occurring. However, none of these efforts would equalize incomes or provide a totally equitable society.

- Conservatives stereotypically oppose aspects of the welfare state; however, it is important to keep in mind that on a worldwide basis, conservatives like British Prime Minister Disraeli and German Prime Minister Bismarck actually started social welfare programs.

- Radicals appear to support more social welfare as an interim measure to help poor and working-class people. There is not much discussion as to what the exact role of social welfare would be under a socialist economy.

Libertarian Issues

A major set of issues divide themselves more along the lines of libertarianism versus social control. The anti-alcohol movement, which succeeded in making booze illegal from 1919 to 1933, was more closely associated with progressives of that time (although not radicals). Drug use and its control were not very controversial until some baby boomers rallied around marijuana legalization, and in recent years, the war on drugs has been critiqued by some on the left and within the African-American community. When the Republican Party was less encumbered by the New Right, they had their civil libertarians as well as the Democrats. Today some libertarians, though hardly all, are Republicans. There are people supportive of the right to choose, to have sex with anyone they choose, and to even criticize the large amount of money going for defense. There are issues today, like the increasing control over diet from controlling sugary drinks to mandating vegetarian food, that make conservatives angry but are supported by some liberals and left-wingers.

Public and Private Ownership

While conservatives often glorify private ownership, it is true that progressive or liberal movements have sought to limit its power over many areas. In some nations, reform groups have prevailed on governments to take over certain industries, but this effort may be criticized by some as "lemon socialism" as it puts only failed industry in government hands, providing a sort of albatross around government's neck. In the US, there has not been a major effort to promote public rather than private ownership, although some liberals and others have protested mass contracting out of government services as a negative and as a disservice to consumers.

Race, Gender, and Sexual Minorities

Like some other issues (see environmental and immigration issues for example), these issues were not central in separating the original progressives from conservatives. Historian Richard Hofstadter has noted how generally anti-immigrant most of the Yankee Protestant leaders of Progressivism were. Some parts of the Progressive base, particularly in the West, did support women's suffrage. Even into the 1930s and 1940s, there was not a huge interest in these issues within the Democratic Party although rights for African-Americans were an issue for communists and progressives. Still, in 1964, the Civil Rights Act passed with as much Republican as Democratic Party votes, keeping in mind most of the South was governed by Dixiecrat Democrats. In the 1960s–1980s, voting shifted tremendously with much of the Southern whites moving to support the Republican Party while African-Americans as well as white liberals supporting civil rights supported the Democrats. The women's movement, which began in the 1960s, and like the New Left was outside the established parties, came like the people of color to find a more willing audience for abortion rights, equal pay for women, civil rights, and other reforms with liberal Democrats. At first, this was unclear as moderate Republicans, including Richard Nixon and Gerald Ford, supported the Equal Rights Amendment and other reform proposals. The rise of the New Right and their increased control of the GOP also meant, as a reaction, many groups who advocated efforts to support women and people of color and then gay and lesbian people supported the Democrats.

Radicals have adopted complete support to identity movements in most cases and in some cases such as reparations for African-Americans to go further in the policy debate.

TWO

The Original Progressives: "The Radical Movement Under Conservative Direction"

The most prominent historian of the first Progressive movement, Richard Hofstadter (1960, 1963), quoted approvingly the title (above) of the lecture Theodore Roosevelt gave to businessmen. It illustrates well the paradox of the rather heterogeneous group of reformers in the first two decades of the twentieth century: a radical voice for conservative ends. On the one hand, several prominent people involved in the Progressive era verged on radicalism, most notably settlement house leader Jane Addams and Wisconsin Governor and Senator Robert La Follette, particularly in their anti-war stands. But for the most part, the reform effort was led by fairly conservative people such as Republican President Theodore Roosevelt (1901–1909) and later a progressive-come-lately Democratic President Woodrow Wilson (1913–1921) who steered the era in at best a mild reformist bent. They intentionally hoped to spearhead the reform movement along rather limited lines as opposed to the radicals who appeared strong at this time (see below).

It is best to see the unrest of the era being a bit of a three-ring circus with spontaneous journalistic revelations from the muckrakers at the beginning of the twentieth century; second, the growth of the left, which created great fear among the wealthy and the middle class, including Progressives; and finally, the organized political response centered first in the Republican Party and later in both parties, which sought to contain the unrest in a manageable way. Along the way in 1912, Roosevelt, having failed to take over his own party (the Republican Party), ran as a Progressive (also known as the Bull Moose Party), which received nearly 28 percent of the vote; but he was defeated by the Democrat Wilson. I will treat separately an entirely different Progressive Party, that of 1924, later in the chapter. (See table 2 for a list of the three major Progressive parties in US history and an addition of campaigns that could be considered in their historical vein.)

Context

The turn of the twentieth century found the United States a nation that, unlike its past, was increasingly urban and industrialized. In many ways, neither the government structure nor its regulation of industry had kept up with the times. America was ruled by laissez-faire capitalist ideas, and the great industrialization that followed the Civil War had led to corrupt monopolies, destruction of environments, overcrowding, poverty, and oppressive conditions for the predominantly immigrant (as well as native) working class, as well as teeming slums of the poor. (None of this mentions the genocide of Native Americans or the enslavement and Jim Crow semi-enslavement of African-Americans). Politically, neither party had a great deal of interest in those at or near the bottom of society. The Republicans were the party of industry and elites, generally hostile to labor and new white ethnic immigrants. Yet they were supported by most African-Americans who were allowed to vote and also by the middle-class voters in the West and Northeast. But the Democratic Party, while inclusive of many immigrant voters, were run by boss-machines in big cities and by the Dixiecrat white segregationists in the South. Both parties focused their energy in the cultural fights of the time such as the battle to outlaw drinking, creating the "drys" and "wets." The Republicans were more "dry," and the Democrats more wet. Temperance along with the tariff and the money supply (William Jennings Bryan's call for moving off the gold standard, for example) was the major issue. Neither party took up ways to seriously represent or assist the poorer classes nor to control the power of newly ascendant businessmen.

Of course, there had been protests and many violent conflicts before, "as American as apple pie" as H. Rap Brown once said. To name only a few, the 1877 rail strikes, which in some parts of the nation neared a complete general strike, came close to shutting down the country. In 1886, strikes for the eight-hour day rocked the country and led to the famous Haymarket Riot in Chicago in which a bomb went off in the square killing several people, and the anarchists were blamed, leading to the arrest of eight and the hanging of four people. In 1894, a huge confrontation followed the Pullman Strike led by Eugene V. Debs (see below), which also caused a national crisis. Meanwhile, beginning in the 1890s, an agrarian rebellion known as the Populist Movement gathered strength in most of the nation west of the Mississippi and parts of the South. Interestingly, quite a few reforms claimed as progressive in the twentieth century were taken from populism.

The protests and strikes of the late nineteenth century were often brutally put down. One of the key differences between the Progressive period and earlier days was the eventual willingness of some elites to accept certain reforms as a compromise while rejecting any radical ideas put forward. In 1902, Theodore Roosevelt signaled a new mood when he decided to arbitrate an important anthracite mine workers strike rather than simply repress it. The same year, TR got his reputation (far overblown) as a trust-buster by intervening in the case of the Northern Securities Company when the JPMorgan interests attempted to take it over. As Hofstadter notes (1960, p. 235), these were symbolic actions, but they marked a period in which federal intervention was no longer a dirty word, and some of it could be at least neutral and not pro-corporate.

Muckrakers

Many historians speak of the Progressive movement as a middle-class movement, and no sector was an important part of it more than the new journalists, magazine writers, and freelancers in the major cities. Two magazines, *McClure's* and the *American Magazine*, were particularly noted for their investigative pieces. The most famous muckrakers included Ida Tarbell whose exposé, <u>*The History*</u>

of the Standard Oil Company, revealed the tremendous corruption in building the nation's largest monopoly (1904); Upton Sinclair's *The Jungle*, a graphic representation of the horrors of the meatpacking industry of the time (1906); Lincoln Steffens's *The Shame of the Cities* (1904), which uncovered the corruption of several political machines in major cities; and Frank Norris's *The Octopus* (1901), which is actually a novel that revealed the entanglement of corrupt railroads and ranchers and other prominent interests in California. Ironically, the negative label *muckraker* was given to the journalists by none other than Theodore Roosevelt. The radical analyses of some of America's most powerful groups did not sit well with him. He accused the muckrakers of being "friends of disorder" who mucked the dirt from the ground. He said of Upton Sinclair, "I have an utter contempt for him" (both quotes from Kolko, p. 110).

Importantly, while the muckrakers brought great publicity to the issues of public and big-business corruption, malfeasance, and awful conditions faced by workers and consumers and helped lay the ground for the era being called progressive, they themselves often considered the remedies too mild and even just-for-show responses. Upton Sinclair thought the well-known Pure Food and Drug Act passed by Congress in 1906 was totally deficient in terms of the issues he raised. Historian Gabriel Kolko reported Sinclair "opposed the bill from start and called for municipal slaughterhouses." He also wrote, "Nobody even pretends to believe that I improved the condition of the stockyard workers" (pp. 105, 107). But muckrakers could only disclose an issue or set of issues and get people excited perhaps only for a short time; they were often unable to steer how legislators and executives in the political system handled the issues.

Radicals

If one stool of Progressivism was the muckrakers, a major background and cause of Progressivism was the emergence of strong working-class protests and increased support for socialism. As a percentage of the nation, more people supported socialism in the first decades of the twentieth century than they did in the Great Depression or in the 1960s and 1970s, at least as far as we can tell by votes or party members.

The Socialist Party led ably by the charismatic Eugene V. Debs, who first came to fame as head of the American Railway Union (ARU), was slowly building up a following as the years went by. While certainly strong among some immigrants—Jews, Germans, and Finnish, for example— unlike earlier leftist movements, they had a strong native-born following as well. In 1912, Debs reached 6 percent of the vote, securing nearly a million votes—the highest for a socialist or similarly named party in US history. In 1920, he even ran from prison where he had been jailed for his anti-war activity opposing World War I and still received 3.4 percent of the vote. The Socialists also elected two members of Congress (Meyer London in New York City and Victor Berger in Milwaukee), seventy mayors in total, and many state legislators and city councilors.

Meanwhile, a radical syndicalist organization, the Industrial Workers of the World, formed in 1905. Syndicalism was a form of radical unionism, which believed workers could run not only their factories or offices but also their nations if organized in syndicates, drawing on the work of the French theorist Georges Sorel. The IWW organized where other unions feared to go and heroized strike militancy, working-class militancy generally, and led free speech fights when they were attacked. Several martyrs of the IWW were created, such as singer Joe Hill who was hanged in Utah in 1915, blamed for the death of a grocer. The biggest strikes of the IWW occurred in Lawrence, Massachusetts, (the so-called Bread and Roses Strike) in which they led thousands of textile workers of all ethnicities in a long battle to form a union; in Paterson, New Jersey, among the silk workers in 1913 where New York City's

Madison Square Garden was used for a huge rally; and ironworkers in the Mesabi Range in Minnesota (1916)— the biggest strike in that state. Although initiated by the Western Federation of Miners (which had been a part of the IWW), the bloody massacre at Ludlow, Colorado, in 1914 also had a dramatic impact on public opinion. Historians judge this as one of the bloodiest battles in labor history when National Guard troops protecting Rockefeller-owned property attacked unarmed families camped out in tents, shooting and burning children and women. This strike and battle were such an embarrassment; it led to congressional hearings that urged reforms (see particularly Boyer and Marais 1975, Dubofsky 1969, and Zinn 2015)

While one can always dispute the size and potential of the radicals in the United States at the time, there is little doubt that their presence was constantly on the mind of the Progressives. The following two quotes serve as examples:

1906 Roosevelt wrote to William Howard Taft "the corruption of business" had led "to unhealthy condition of excitement and irritation in the popular mind, which shows itself in part in the enormous increases in the socialistic propaganda." (cited in Hofstadter, p. 239)

1912 George W. Perkins, fundraiser for the Republican Party and then Progressive Party: "Perkins was concerned with the growth of the Socialist vote and 'rapidly approaching crisis in this country on the question of the relation between capital and labor and business and the State.'" (Kolko and citation in Kolko, p. 192)

A major factor in all the political activities of the Progressives was to limit the damage they felt radicals and socialists might do to both the political and the socioeconomic system. This does not mean there was never cooperation between the groups. Because of the diversity of the Progressive movement, several individuals who moved leftward sometimes ended up in alliances with radicals.

Progressives: Who They Were

Historians of the Progressive era agree that the reformers were middle class in nature. Some of the leaders Hofstadter notes many of the leaders were

"leading Progressive politicians were very often from well-established families, the sons of well-to-do professionals or business men who were inspired by the high civic ideals kept alive since the Civil War." (Hofstadter 1963, p. 7)

The reformers go back to what were called the Mugwumps—a middle- to upper-class group of reformers within the Republican Party who were more liberal than the leadership of the later nineteenth century. Hofstadter further notes that

"middle class in leadership, they were 'almost pathetically respectable'… William Allen White surveying the Bull Moose movement saw 'it as petit bourgeois a movement of little businessmen, professional men, well-to-do farmers, skilled artisans from the upper brackets of organized labor.'" (Hofstadter, pp. 131–132)

Importantly, they were also

"almost entirely native-born Protestants, [they] had extraordinarily high representative of professional men and college graduates. The rest were businessmen, proprietors of fairly large enterprises." (Hofstadter, p. 132, quoting White)

Robert Wiebe agrees that

"the heart of program was the ambition of the new middle class to fulfill its destiny through bureaucratic means ... its epicenter was large cities of East and Midwest and predominantly agrarian states of Midwest. "(Wiebe 1967, p. 166)

Because of the class and ethnic composition, the Progressives were, in modern terms, both liberal and conservative. Hofstadter saw the middle class as feeling "squeezed":

"between both the emergence of a small but (also) vigorous labor movement ad in the trustification of American industry ... some Progressives saw the United States (as) heading towards, on one side corporate paternalism, and, on the other

side, to state socialism-both (being) fatal
to individual liberties." (Hofstadter 1960,
pp. 169, 224)

As we shall see, as middle-class Yankee reformers, the Progressives were sometimes hostile to the working and lower classes. They tended to see lower-class immigrants as in the grips of the party bosses and hence, in need of paternal intervention and supervision. The substitution of the mayoral and city council system by a city manager system, for example, favored by many Progressives, was an undemocratic attempt to bring expertise to government by avoiding the electoral process. Many Progressives supported banning alcohol particularly from the hands of the poor and the mob. They split on issues of labor unions, preferring regulatory policies that were in the middle, so to speak, of the range between labor and capital and left and right.

Progressives: Issue Consensus and Conflict

To be fair, it is hard to generalize about the Progressives totally. As Nancy C. Unger notes in her biography of Robert La Follette,

"the complexity of the Progressive movement is exacerbated by the diversity of programs it encompassed ... some [reformers] supported only one reform ... some a
full slate of reforms." (Unger 1988, p.121)

Another major complexity is that the Progressive
movement was far more influential on a state level than on
a national level. This was due, on the one hand, not only
to the more homogenous nature of some states than the
whole nation but also of the lesser complexities of navigating state legislatures and governors compared to the federal
system of checks and balances. For example, Wisconsin
under both the governorship of La Follette and his successors as well as California led by Hiram Johnson saw most
of (at least the less controversial) Progressive reforms pass.
Often the Progressives could not muster this support across
the nation in Congress.

Two types of issues were generally supported by
almost all Progressives: One was an assortment of political
reforms, which were popular going back to the Populists,
that Progressives believed would help change the political
system. The second were efforts to regulate the economy
by law or, more often, by a neutral commission or board,
which could be a watchdog for the people.

On the political front, the Progressives hoped to defeat both the local bosses and the party bosses by increasing the democratic participation of the people. They bemoaned how closed politics was, as was true even more then than now. Senators were elected by state legislatures; meaning, someone who was not tied in with the dominant political powers had little chance of ever being a senator. Equally problematic were party primaries. They were often not open but run by bosses, and hence, the reformers favored direct primaries with direct election to the two parties' national conventions. The addition of recall, referendum, and initiative, which was a major demand of the Populists, was also favored by the Progressives. They believed that the ability of the people to directly propose political change through an initiative or referendum could upend the bosses and the entrenched power interests and that recall could succeed in taking out of power particularly unsavory characters. In a very modern demand—which Robert La Follette, for example, championed—the Progressives call to get money out of politics by banning campaign money being given to political contenders. Still, these democratic plans did not stop Progressives from also championing the city manager system and, in an effort that now seems less noble than it did then, the protective legislation for women and children. The latter reforms came about because of the widespread existence of child labor and long hours for them and the many women who had started to work. In the early twentieth century, most feminists and Progressives favored such actions as they were shocked by the presence of women and children particularly in the factories, mines, and smelters. Today feminists and other reformers favor reforms to be cross-gender, not protective in a paternalist way of preventing women from working at certain places or industries. They did call for abolition of child labor, too, but this would not succeed until well into the New Deal in 1938 with the Fair Labor Standards Act.

If there was a quintessential Progressive reform, it can be labeled regulatory reform. On the federal level, the Progressives expanded the Interstate Commerce Commission (ICC) in 1906, the same year the Pure Food and Drug Act passed. In 1914, under Woodrow Wilson, they succeeded in passing the Federal Trade Commission (FTC) to protect consumers. They grumbled, however, about their failure to ever enact stronger antitrust laws as they were annoyed by the failure of the Sherman Antitrust Act of 1890 to actually forestall or break up monopolies. Though interestingly, it was used against labor unions as being "combinations." Perhaps the most successful but still ambiguous reform of the Progressives was the workman's (now workers') compensation laws passed in the many states at the time.

Like the federal or local commissions and boards, workers' compensation appealed to Progressives as a way to help the poor and injured (and later disabled) workers while not hurting corporations at the same time. As critics on the left have noted (Kolko 1963 and Weinstein 1968), workmen's compensation was in the interest of the major companies. What had occurred in the nineteenth century was because of the lack of any coverage for injured workers, the only way a worker or, often, his or her surviving family could obtain justice was to sue in the local courts for damages. Indeed, they did, and the damage claims in some cases were beginning to be astounding. More than that, for the newly grown large corporation, the failure to be able to plan a budget for such costs was an enormous inconvenience. While small companies might have tried to make do without any state intervention, large companies favored workmen's compensation because it was a relatively small amount of money, which was predictable over the years (and capped at a certain amount for each injury or death). Moreover, controversies could be shifted from the companies to the state; and indeed, today many grievances about workers' compensation claims go on for years. But workers and their families blame the government for their bureaucracy and mean-spiritedness, often not the company that caused their accident.

Corporate support for antitrust action and federal and state boards also did not sway Progressives from supporting them. To the Progressives, these reforms were no-brainers in that they helped some people while not enflaming further class conflict. To large companies who were busy hiring the best attorneys and, later, public relations firms, they were fairly well able to handle the increased costs of regulations, while often they found their competitors unable to. Kolko argues, for example, "that [while] monopoly became a political slogan for small merchant, beleaguered farmer, and unemployed worker," it was the large companies that lobbied Congress and presidents Roosevelt, Taft, and Wilson in the era to pass laws. These corporations not only had big pockets but also had tremendous influence with the government. They did not fear government intervention, and particularly, when it did not disturb their own corporation, they were all in favor of it (Kolko 1963, pp. 62–4).

Although there were many areas of disagreement between Progressives, three good examples of conflict were the attitudes they maintained on labor unions, on civil rights for minorities (especially people of color), and on foreign policy and war.

In theory, many Progressives supported the working person's right to organize. However, where unions they succeeded, Progressives often demurred full support for unions, fearing they would become powerful. Herbert Croly, one of the main theorists of the Progressives, wrote scathingly in 1909 that some unions were "arrogant and lawless." He wrote that

> "the most serious danger to the American democratic future which may issue from aggressive and unscrupulous unionism consists in the state of mind of which mob violence is one example." (document 19, Hofstadter 1963)

Croly went on to equate labor and industry

> "as occupying similar relations ... both are so powerful ... frequently too strong for the state government, and in different ways they both traffic for their own benefit with politicians." (ibid.)

Because the Progressives were committed to the familiar liberal belief in a neutral public and state above the interests of each section, Croly could not see unions (or any other forms) as representing large segments of the public. Moreover, at a time when great battles were fought usually only when strikebreakers were employed or the police or National Guard were brought in, it was a bit unfair to blame unions for mob violence.

Even Louis Brandeis, the liberal jurist who was an active Progressive and was later appointed by Woodrow Wilson to the Supreme Court, differed from labor in many ways. Brandeis and Samuel Gompers, the leader of the AFL (American Federation of Labor), differed on several important issues, including the effort to make unions incorporate so they could be sued, the closed shop, and most tellingly, Taylorism. That Brandeis and many Progressives were enamored of the new scientific management of the 1910s led by Frederick Winslow Taylor is telling in itself. Progressives worshipped expertise and believed in efficiency. Hence, they saw Taylor's time-motion studies and efforts to replace as much labor as possible as a Progressive cause. The labor leaders responded that Brandeis was endorsing a speedup on the factory lines and a way to cut down the workforce (see Urofosky 2009, pp. 228–245 on Brandeis and labor).

Civil rights were not a central issue to Progressives. But the most liberal, such as Jane Addams and Robert La Follette, were most consistent in supporting women's suffrage, Indian rights, complete equality for African-Americans, and other issues. Roosevelt was silent on women's suffrage until the 1912 election. When running as a Progressive for president, he suddenly called Addams, endorsed suffrage, and asked her to nominate him at the convention, which she did (see Knight 2010 and also Chace 2004). Woodrow Wilson, however, remained opposed; and the Democrats came to support women's suffrage only after the world war.

Addams clashed several times with Roosevelt over civil rights. In 1906, she clashed with him over his immigration bill that included a literacy test sure to remove many non-Anglo immigrants from eligibility for immigration and also proposed a ban on some Asian immigrants. She was able to secure Democratic Party support, which opposed the bill, and got the literacy test thrown out (it would later come back in the restrictive legislation passed in the 1920s). But Roosevelt held to banning Japanese laborers, as California industrialists had proposed (see Knight, pp. 140–143). In 1912, when Addams had already endorsed Roosevelt, he refused to have an integrated convention and rejected the proposed civil rights plank put forward by the NAACP (National Association for the Advancement of Colored People) of which Addams was a board member.

A biographer says Addams "came very close to bolting the Progressive Party" over the issue (Knight, pp. 174–176).

No issue led to such isolation for the few Progressives who were anti-war than foreign policy. Hofstadter noted that Addams and La Follette aside

> "the main stream of feeling in the ranks of insurgency was neither anti-war nor anti-imperialist. Its real spiritual leader, in this as in other respects, was Theodore Roosevelt with his military preachments and his hearty appeals to unselfish patriotism." (1960, p. 274)

Robert La Follette was an important exception. Initially, he supported the administration; but in the aftermath of TR's gunboat diplomacy and bullying the nations of Latin America, he changed his thinking and became a consistent opponent of the bipartisan foreign policy. For example, he demanded the Philippines become independent (Addams was far ahead of him here as she joined the American Anti-Imperialist League during the Spanish-American War in 1899), he denounced Wilson's battles with and intervention in Mexico, and he saw profit for industry as behind the US policy in Latin America (Unger, p. 236).

The growing strength of the war fever after the break-out of war in Europe in 1914 stunned both Addams and La Follette, who urged a popular referendum on any war plans. Addams created several peace organizations and worked with Europeans to prevent war. However, they did not succeed. Both suffered the incredible isolation when the United States entered the war in 1917. Addams was booed frequently at talks and was later thrown out of the Daughters of the American Revolution (DAR) for her pacifism, but she later was awarded the first Nobel Peace Prize for a woman in 1931 many years after the war. La Follette was attacked in the papers and in cartoons portraying him as a Hun and a traitor. Indeed, Roosevelt himself called him "a shadow Hun" and "the most dangerous political leader [of] the analogue to the Bolshevik agitation" (Unger, p. 255). La Follette was humiliated when his former allies at the University of Wisconsin (with whom he worked closely as governor) turned on him, and the faculty voted 421–2 to denounce him in 1917 and expressed "their grief and shame" in him (Unger, p. 257).

From Progressives to the Progressive Party of 1924

It is necessary to at least briefly treat the Progressive Party, formed in 1924 to contest the presidential election that year a bit separately. The Progressive era, by almost unanimous historical view, ended in the depths of the World War I. Few of the original leaders were left, and many went quietly off to support militarism. By the war's aftermath, despite a huge strike wave in the nation that idled one of five workers, the country moved to the political right. In part, in fact, because of the labor unrest and fears of radicalism, a nationwide sweep called the Palmer Raids was ordered, rounding up thousands of supposed radicals, particularly those who were immigrants. Of course, Addams and La Follette protested, but they were in a small minority. The 1920s would be known as a return to normalcy and the prosperous roaring '20s. Warren Harding and Calvin Coolidge, among the most conservative presidents, took over.

It was somewhat an accident of history that created space briefly for a second Progressive Party. One factor was La Follette's own political ambitions and ego, which, according to a biographer, were mammoth. In every presidential year since 1912, La Follette geared up to run for president (Unger, p.184); and after all, Roosevelt had snatched what would have been his run in 1912 by taking the first Progressive Party run. But the major reason was a complete deadlock at the Democratic Convention of 1924 that produced one of the most embarrassing splits and poor nominees the party has seen. Two political forces, one representing the more Eastern ethnic wing behind Alfred E. Smith, battled furiously with William G. McAdoo, who represented the more rural and Midwestern and Southern parts of the party. The party split with two key issues being the KKK (Ku Klux Klan), which had reached the zenith of its national following in the early 1920s, and the Prohibition issue. The convention deadlocked for 102 ballots with McAdoo forces supporting Prohibition and KKK and with Smith calling for end to Prohibition and for a condemnation of the KKK. On the 103rd ballot, the Democrats nominated a little-known corporate lawyer John W. Davis. Davis was not a choice for any even mild liberal; he was a representative of big corporate interests and a laissez-faire proponent.

The very-hastily-called-into-being party differed from the previous Progressive efforts not only that La Follette was more toward the left but also that the Progressive Party of 1924 was a labor-farmer-socialist party that married briefly the labor movement of the AFL, the Socialist Party, the old Populist groups, and others. It captured rather well-known supporters such as W. E. B. Du Bois (the African-American leader and scholar who had become an ally of La Follette as well as Jane Addams), Progressive and Socialist Florence Kelley, educator and philosopher John Dewey, and the famous blind figure Helen Keller. Unfortunately, as McKay (1947) well illustrates, the alliance was uneasy. Labor had a policy for decades under Samuel Gompers to "reward its friends and punish its enemies"—a phrase he interpreted as not allying with any party. The idea of a labor party, as many European nations had, was an anathema to him, but popular on the left. Gompers felt trapped by the Democrats' moves and allowed the support of La Follette to go forward, but support was tepid, frequently breaking into hostility toward the Socialists. And it did not prevent numerous local unions from not campaigning at all for La Follette or even for the opposing candidates.

The 1924 party platform can be criticized in several ways. It amazingly avoided the two issues that separated the Democrats, condemning the Klan and a position on Prohibition. Also, as Unger points out, while La Follette had pressed for the US to recognize the Soviet Union, the platform was silent on any issue related to this (p. 290). Still, on the whole, the platform as well as containing some of the usual issues discussed by Progressives went a bit further. It called for a nationalization of the railroads and waterpower systems with democratic management. It called for high taxes on wealth and income and reduction of taxes that fell on the common people. It called for popular election of judges and the abolition of the injunction that had crippled labor's ability to strike. It had an extensive paragraph condemning the foreign policy of the last number of presidents and urged the Versailles Treaty be renegotiated so it did not punish nations, which of course would, in part, lead to World War II (see Progressive Party platform). The platform was prescient in many ways: It called for the paying of the bonus promised to US veterans, which would cause a massive Bonus March in Washington, DC, in 1932. Its call for an end of the injunction presaged the Norris-LaGuardia Act of 1932, and its call for public works during depressions presaged the 1930s programs.

The party was hampered throughout its short life by lack of funds and the inability to even secure ballot status in many states. Because the Socialist Party had ballot access in forty-four states, in some states, voting for La Follette was only possible on a Socialist line (which obviously some people were loath to do), while other states had the Progressive Party and others, an independent status. Given all this, the achievement of nearly five million votes or almost 17 percent of the voters probably should be considered an achievement, even though with our electoral college system, La Follette won only one state, his own, Wisconsin. Some have even called it "the most successful leftwing Presidential campaign in American history" (Gillespie 1993, quoted in Unger, p. 291). Like its predecessor, the 1912 Party, the party vanished quickly; and La Follette died in 1925.

Why All the Fuss? The Limited Accomplishments of the Progressives

Interestingly, the Progressives did not accomplish much. As Hofstadter put it, the "immediate material achievement was quite small in proportion to all the noise" (1960, p. 256). Wiebe adds the "Progressive reform lived largely on tomorrow's hope even at the peak of its national influence" (Wiebe 1967, p. 169).

Compared to even the Populists, as Hofstadter notes, Progressives were more moderate and less original:

> "Progressive thought was more informed, more moderate, more complex than Populist thought had been ... [but] Progressives did not, as a rule, have the daring or originative force of the Populists

of the 1890s and that a great deal of Progressive political effort was spent enacting proposals that the Populists had outlined fifteen or even twenty years earlier." (Hofstadter 1960, pp. 133–134)

Clearly, from the vantage point of history, the changes in the first two decades of the twentieth century are dwarfed by later periods of social unrest led by generally poorer groups. In the early to mid-1930s, the Great Depression and the unrest that spread through much of the poorer populations led to the beginnings of the American welfare state (such as it is), the recognition of union rights and other labor demands, and the development of an infrastructure of much of the modern state from the FDIC (Federal Deposit Insurance Corporation) to the SEC (Securities and Exchange Commission). In the 1960s, the civil rights movement and then the ghetto riots that followed, along with (to a lesser degree) the anti-war and other movements, made for major changes from the Civil Rights Act and the Voting Rights Act to the war on poverty to Medicare and Medicaid to an assortment of policies passed in the early 1970s (Occupational Safety and Health Act, the Clean Air Act, environmental protection, indexing of Social Security benefits, the creation and expansion of food stamps, and almost a passage of a guaranteed income).

Why did the groups and individuals we will discuss in chapters 3, 4 and 5 echo the banner of Progressivism in the 1930s and 1940s and then at least since the 1980s to today? There is not one indisputable answer, and political slogans and names are not rational but chosen to evoke emotion.

Progressives had (and have) three attributes that were not present in other labels. First, they were reformist, not radical or revolutionary. Socialist, Marxist, anarchist, etc. are labels that may be popular elsewhere, but they have always had only small amount of support in the United States. Even La Follette, the most radical of the progressives, was anti-communist and, as Unger quotes from *Collier's* magazine, was a reformist:

> "He is perfectly antique in his view of the Republic. He has nothing in common with the radicals who sneer at the forefathers and who see no difference between the republic of George Washington and any other 'capitalistic' state. La Follette thinks there is a difference. He thinks there is such a thing as Americanism.

He imagines himself to be trying to put
it back into the American government."
(Unger, p. 2)

Jane Addams was quite similar. Though a committed pacifist and a feminist in the first wave style of the movement, she never saw herself as a socialist or any kind of radical; and while allied with the Progressive Party in 1912 and 1924, she voted faithfully for Wilson in 1916 (to her great unhappiness afterward) and in her last year of life for Franklin Roosevelt (Knight, p. 210, 261).

First, the name *progressive* conveys reform within the system, not revolution or radicalism. Second, as we have noted, progressives were a respectable middle-class group. Even nonrevolutionary groups of reformers such as the Populists are not acceptable to those who carry on the name *progressive*. They not only like to be in the company of writers, journalists, professors, scientists, physicians, social workers, psychologists, and other higher-status people but also tend to disdain lower-class movements. One example was Populism itself who, as Hofstadter notes, were the reformers "branded ... as madmen" before adopting their program (Hofstadter 1960, p. 132). They did not like the heated style of Populism, its radical rhetoric, and its threats to turn farmers and poor Westerners loose on the nation.

Interestingly, the Townsend movement of the 1930s is another example of what was a mass movement, but it was not suitable for progressives. Despite being founded by a physician in Long Beach, California, and gaining millions of supporters throughout the nation, liberal historians tend to disdain the movement in part because of its class status and in part because Townsend did not support Roosevelt. A recent book (Mulloy 2018) even places Townsend and Huey Long's Share the Wealth campaign on the right wing presumably because they were low-class and not in harmony with the New Deal (any antagonism to Franklin Roosevelt seems to be equated with not being politically or historically correct). Third, progressives are taken with optimism. Hofstadter noted that

> "the distinguishing thing about Progressives might be called activism: they argued that social evils will not remedy themselves, and that it is wrong to sit by passively and wait for time to take care of them …. [They were] intensely optimistic … [they had] confidence of faith that no problem is too difficult to be overcome by the proper mobilization of energy and intelligence in the citizenry." (1963, p. 5)

Such optimism is a characteristic of progressives. Perhaps it is tied in their reformist and middle-class status. Most poor and working-class people tend to have less faith in the state as an entity and the political system as affectatious.

Although, as we shall see, there is a considerable difference between groups that would emerge carrying the progressive banner, all were reformists, and they believed trying (often the same strategies over and over again) would eventually succeed. Their optimism was reinforced by their own status not only professionally but also in state bureaucracies or social movements (for example, leading labor bureaucrats of the 1930s or leaders of activist or semi-activist nonprofit groups tend to love the term *progressive*).

Table II
Progressive Party in National Presidential Elections

Year	Candidate	Vote and States Carried
1912	Theodore Roosevelt	Nearly 28 percent of vote, eight states carried
1924	Robert La Follette	Nearly 17 percent of vote, one state carried
1948	Henry Wallace	About 2.3 percent of vote, no states carried

Semi-Progressive Runs*

1980	John	About 6.9 percent,
1996, 2000,	Anderson	no state carried
2004, 2008	Ralph	Highest in 2000, 2.7 percent
	Nader	of vote, no states carried

- Neither of these were Progressive parties in name, but they drew on the term and its tradition to different degrees.

THREE

Progressives II: Fellow Travelers of Stalinism

Something different happened to progressives in the 1930s and 1940s. While the New Deal emerged with a fuller blown embodiment of liberalism, *progressivism*, as a term, seemed overshadowed until the help of the Communist Party USA. The word emerged again as allies or fellow travelers of the party, usually nonmembers who attended certain meetings and rallies, signed petitions, and gave their names to calls to action or protest. The change was not formally announced, but the period of 1936–1948 was dominated by calls to the progressive people of the United States (and sometimes the world). Though the Communist Party never had more than one hundred thousand members (if that) and was far more present in places like New York and Los Angeles than in the American heartland, it reached many people through favorable press coverage (at least in the years prior to and during the World War II) and through several front organizations, particularly in the late 1930s. The success of the party came to a grinding halt in 1939 with the Hitler-Stalin Pact, but when the Soviets entered the war in 1941, the Grand Alliance (the United States and Soviet Union) produced some space for solidarity with the party. Gradually from 1945 to 1948, as the Cold War emerged, fewer progressives supported the party; and in 1948, the third Progressive Party running Henry Wallace fared poorly, setting the stage for the full repression of anyone called pink during the McCarthy period.

I will review briefly the complexity of political terms such as liberalism and progressivism, the context of the 1930s and 1940s, and then move on to the Communist Party's Popular Front strategy and its relation to progressives, and then the backlash that occurred by the late 1940s against communism. Those labeled progressives once again showed amazing levels of naivete and optimism as Stalin built his totalitarian regime while accepting the status quo of capitalism in the United States.

What's in a Name?

One of the few authors to address political labels is David Green in his *The Language of Politics in America*

(1988). Green notes the language of politics is fluid and flexible and may even come in overlapping one another (those who call themselves more than one thing). For many years, at least in the 1910s and 1920s, it appears *progressive* and *liberal* competed with each other. Woodrow Wilson, Green notes, "gradually moved from progressive to liberal" (p.76), and Herbert Hoover, while regarded by many as a conservative today, "successfully identified as both 'progressive' and 'liberal'" (p. 5). Franklin Roosevelt was most concerned about painting his enemies as conservatives or, better yet, reactionaries. As time went on, FDR moved from using *progressive* to *liberal* in his speeches.

One issue was in the 1930s, the Progressive movement was close enough in history that many people would regard statements containing that name as specific to the parties of Theodore Roosevelt and then Robert La Follette. But in fact, as Green points out (p. 123), many old Progressives did not favor the New Deal. While we really have no empirical data, we must treat as persuasive, at least tentatively, that "on balance [they] disapproved of the New Deal," seeing it as "coercive and confiscatory." FDR seemed to have taken umbrage at this and limited his term to *liberal*. Second, Green notes that FDR liked *liberal* as a flexible symbol that could minimize resistance as "it connoted freedom as well as generosity" (p. 122). As many have noted, *progres-*

sive is a directional term, describing a process rather than a more set term, which the New Deal sought to define with a more interventionist state providing social welfare as well as financial stability.

None of this fully answers how the liberals, moderates, and radicals who supported the Popular Front from the mid-1930s on came to be termed *progressives*. We do not fully know if the Communist Party (CP) preferred the term *progressive*, which, all accounts agree, was one of the chief words in their lexicon. Much later, Howe and Coser (p. 470) note that Henry Wallace captured the very essence of Midwestern progressivism and Americanism and hence was a good candidate for the CP-dominated Progressive Party in 1948. It may be that some sympathetic groups already called themselves progressives, that some were referred to as progressive by the party and others, or that given the association of the New Deal with liberalism was seen as taking up the space for this label. After all, in the first half of the 1930s, the Communist Party considered itself a revolutionary party, and being liberal may not have suited their self-concept. By the mid-1930s Popular Front, they wished to sound respectable (but perhaps not supporting the status quo), and hence *progressive* was perhaps malleable enough to cover many views. In any event, since the allies of the Popular Front were known as progressives,

I will call them that while leaving, at this point, the *liberal* term to those (usually Democratic Party officials) who labeled themselves as such.

It should be added though that while all Western societies worshipped progress, *progressive* and *progress* held a particular role in the Marxist dialectic. Since history progressed toward socialism and then communism, to many Marxists and also some progressives, the name could be a way of supporting this process without using the scary term *communist*.

Context

Of course, nothing dominated the 1930s as much as the Great Depression, which is dated from the stock market crash of October 1929. More than one in four people were unemployed at each point in the Depression, and many workers suffered wage cuts. While at first people responded with shock and depression to the massive unemployment, wage cuts, and dire poverty of the times, by 1932, a wave of social unrest had spread across the nation like wildfire. Frances Fox Piven and Richard Cloward's books *Regulating the Poor* (original 1971) and *Poor People's Movements* (1977) are among the best in presenting the unrest of the 1930s. To take only a few examples, in 1932, thousands of veterans marched on Washington, DC, demanding the payment of a bonus promised years earlier by the government—the famous Bonus March. Estimated at about fifteen thousand people quietly surrounded the Capitol, and many took up tents around it. After a period of standoff, the US Army led by Gen. Douglas MacArthur attacked the marchers at the order of President Hoover, burning their shanties and killing and wounding veterans. The nation stood in shock as the Capitol area lay in flames and gunfire.

Beginning in the winter of 1932, groups of unemployed organized around the nation—some organized by the Communist Party, some by the Socialist Party, and some by others such as A. J. Muste (an independent radical). In many cities, the Unemployed Councils marched, and in turn were attacked by police. All over, they helped evicted tenants reclaim their goods and retake their apartments. At a time when there was no social safety net, they demanded the government (federal, state, and local) to respond to the Depression with immediate relief.

At the same time, several other major movements began. Led by a dentist from California, Francis Townsend, petitions and clubs developed all over America, demanding pensions for those over sixty. The Townsend movement gathered millions of signatures at a time long before the internet and social media, the old way by door-to-door work. Huey Long, the popular governor of Louisiana, whose strong ambitions included the White House, began promoting a Share the Wealth campaign under the slogan "Every Man a King!" This plan would have provided a government stipend to all poorer and working people. Only the assassination of Long in 1935 probably prevented Long from trying for the presidency and even possibly threatening Franklin Roosevelt's status. In 1934, a movement in the South began, which united white and black sharecroppers and tenant farmers under the leadership of Socialist Party member Harry Mitchell (see PBS's *Great Depression* series [1993], "Mean Things Happen' in the Land"). The union, the Southern Tenant Farmers Union (STFU), had some success by the mid-1930s, pressuring the Roosevelt administration to give agricultural aid to the sharecroppers themselves, not to the big planters. In 1934, strikes broke out across the nation. The most famous included the Minneapolis trucking strike, which eventually shut down much of business in that state and led to a general strike of all workers in Minneapolis, Minnesota. Led by a Trotskyist group (critical of the Soviet Union's "sellout" of communism), the strike scared much of American business. Then meanwhile in San Francisco, a massive longshoremen's strike shut down the ports of the West Coast and led to a general strike among all workers in San Francisco. This strike made famous West Coast leader Harry Bridges, who became a Communist Party member and activist. Such strikes led to the calling in of the National Guard and sometimes federal troops.

The New Deal so praised by liberals and progressives was actually an attempt to cool down social unrest by granting minimal reforms necessary. The reforms were also greatly less in scope and actual benefit than they were in most European nations with a welfare state. The key reforms were the Social Security Act of 1935, which provided pensions and unemployment insurance and some welfare benefits. The benefits and eligibility for these programs were nowhere in the same universe as demanded by protesters. For example, while the Townsend movement wanted *all* elders to be eligible for pensions, the Social Security Act developed a work eligibility level of ten years, excluding many millions of people (along with not covering whole categories of workers such as agricultural workers, domestic workers, public employees, etc.). Whereas the Townsendites wanted a $200 a month payment, the Social Security payments were based on one's earnings and did not (and still does not) take many families out of poverty. It would be well into the 1940s before a majority of people even received a check. While the Lundeen Bill, sponsored by a Communist Party congressman Ernest Lundeen, would have given aid to *all* the unemployed through the federal government, the New Deal administration and Congress passed, in turn, an unemployment insurance program that excluded millions of workers not in the workforce and/or without prior work credits. It also left the administration to the states, which would have a complex maze of regulations and requirements and would set some of the rates at extremely low levels (while many people receive 50 percent of their prior earnings, in many states, a very low maximum benefit is set).

The New Deal was a hurried and convoluted response to the fears of both business and the incumbent political parties. Roosevelt rushed the Social Security Act in direct reaction to Townsend's movement (Holtzman 1975). Its other major actions so praised—public works programs, the National Labor Relations Act or Wagner Act, and the Fair Labor Standards Act of 1938—were all similarly important but incomplete actions. The public works bills were a hasty response to the unrest of workers throughout the country. The number of jobs never even approached the need for work nor did the low wages ever suffice (Works Progress Administration workers did unionize and fight for better pay and conditions with mixed success). Nor did these actions do much to combat the Depression that continued until the early 1940s when war preparation led to a huge rise in factory orders. The NLRB (the National Labor Relations Board), in response to the strikes and class warfare across the country, outlawed some unfair labor practices used against unions and ensured a legal process for collective bargaining. Like many bills, the Supreme Court was divided on the legality of the new government intervention, and it eventually ruled 5–4 for it. However, history has shown that as soon as unions were weakened, the NLRB meant very little. By the 1970s, unions were losing most elections they participated in; and by the twenty-first century, unions were a small percentage of the workforce. Rather, the NLRB had tied labor to a government bureaucracy; it had an incredible amount of faith in government bureaucracy rather than organizing and mobilizing their own rank and file. So much for the "Magna Carta of labor," as labor leaders, liberals, and progressives called the NLRB. The Fair Labor Standards Act was more straightforward: finally, abolishing child labor, guaranteeing overtime and workdays of eight hours, and setting a minimum wage. The bill finally ended a thirty-year battle over issues like child labor and the workday.

The Popular Front: A Quick Deradicalization

It is always hard to reimagine what history could have been with any success. Perhaps the actions of the Roosevelt administration would have dampened social unrest and radical political views anyway. The power of co-optation is strong in America. People wish to go back to their daily lives; they do not like to protest.[3] Historically, Americans often settle for symbolic change rather than thoroughgoing change. The overwhelming victory of FDR in 1936 over Republican Alfred Landon, who won only two states, along with the poor showings of protest parties (The Union Party won less than 2 percent of the vote, Norman Thomas and his Socialist Party about 0.4 percent, and Earl Browder and the Communist Party only 0.17 percent) both suggest the power of mild reform over radicalism. However, it was also true that significant radicalism and discontent remained on a street and rank-and-file level. One indication was the sit-down strikes of 1937, most famously at the General Motors plants in Flint, Michigan, but carried forward throughout America from offices to small businesses.

In particular, had the Communist Party not moved sharply to the right and backed the Democratic Party for nearly a dozen years, it may have had an effect on the events of the 1930s and 1940s. However, in 1935, the

Soviet Comintern changed the party line in its Seventh Congress.[4] Led by George Dimitroff, the new line ordered all Communist parties to move to a Popular Front in which parties would ally with liberals, social democrats, moderates, and whoever else against the rise of fascism. Of course, the change in line was not without some good cause. During the rise of Nazism in the early 1930s, the Communist parties worldwide, in what was known as the third period, were ultraleftist. They refused alliance with all parties and, in fact, attacked socialist and social democratic parties as "social fascist." The incredible defeat in Germany in the 1930s by Nazism stunned Stalin and the Russian Party who now confronted a rearming Germany not very far from its border. The situation, of course, was worsened by the presence of fascism in Italy, the rise of pro-fascist parties in much of Eastern Europe, and the rise of a militaristic aggressive Japan that would ally with Germany and Italy.

Yet as urgent as fascism as a threat was and as much as a coalition may have been necessary, the declaration of the Popular Front led to a wholesale abandonment of communist politics throughout much of the world. The Socialist Party, for example, had long called for a united front, in which working-class and left-wing parties could unite; but few leftists had envisioned a popular front, which included all who would ally with the Communist Party. Norman Thomas, in fact, said this:

> "How can we have a people's front that will lead to the great cause of the emancipation of the workers if it is to include Democrats and Republicans?" (quoted in Howe and Coser 1962, p. 327)

In fact, the ill-thought-out change of party line went far further in some other countries than the United States. In France, the Communist Party expressed hope that the right-wing volunteers and the Catholic Church would join them; in Greece, the party went from being anti-monarchist to supporting it; and in Italy, the party called for a reconciliation of fascists and non-fascists (see Howe and Coser 1962, pp. 324–5).

In the United States, the aping of patriotic themes was humorous:

> "[At the] party's ninth convention [in] June 1936 across the gallery, flaming red steamers with white letters carried slogans … the unity of labor can crush fascism and prevent war! For a free, happy and pros-

perous America! High in the rear of the
auditorium an immense canvas showed
the spirit of '76- drummer, fife, stan-
dard-bearer-carrying red and American
flags intertwined. Out of these emerged
the faces of Washington, Jefferson, John
Brown, Lincoln, Frederick Douglass;
beneath them the slogan: 'Communism is
twentieth-century Americanism.'" (cited
in Klehr 1984, p. 191)

In New York the next year, the Communist Party caught
the conservative Daughters of the American Revolution
(DAR) napping.

"It neglected to celebrate the 162nd anni-
versary of Paul Revere's ride. But the
Young Communist League did not for-
get. It hired a horse and rider dressed in
Continental costume to prance up and
down Broadway with a sign proclaiming
'The DAR Forgets, But the YCL (Young
Communist League) remembers!'"

But the deradicalization was not funny when one includes the Stalinization of the left that occurred at this time. Dwight Macdonald—briefly a CP member, who broke with them in 1937 and was an editor of *Partisan Review*, which favored Trotskyism—describes the liberals (e.g., progressives as well) as "totalitarian liberals" who had a "moral atrophy" (cited in Howe and Coser 1962, p. 435). These liberals/progressives were admirers of industrialization and centralization of the Soviet Union and were awed by its power. Take these examples of deep problems with 1930/1940s communism:

- At the very time of the Popular Front, the Soviet Union was having its show trials, which convicted almost all the remaining Bolsheviks of treason and Trotskyism. It was the beginning of the purge that would affect millions of people in the Soviet Union (of course, this is not to mention the deaths of millions in the earlier collectivization campaign). While a few people active with the CP dropped out of the party in response to the Moscow Trials, including writers John Dos Passos and Mary McCarthy, while writer Waldo Frank (a leader of the front organization League of American Writers) was pushed out because of his questioning of Moscow's line (Ottanelli 1991, p. 167), most progressives shrugged their shoulders. The *Nation* and the *New Republic*, two central organs of progressive thought,[5] were silent on the purges and murders (Ottanelli 1991, p.168). In 1938, a large number of fellow travelers signed a letter supporting the Moscow Trials. These included writer Malcolm Cowley, actor John Garfield, writer Theodore Dreiser, writers Dashiell Hammett and Lillian Hellman, poet Langston Hughes, and critic Dorothy Parker, to name a few (ibid., p. 167). One wonders if after the revolutionary war, a trial had convicted Washington, Jefferson, and Adams of treason and executed them, whether there would a little suspicion among supporters of the revolution! Whether the CP and its supporters were blind or guilty of cynicism is really not clear.

- The Spanish Civil War became one of the key causes of the late 1930s when fascist Generalissimo Franco attacked the elected Republican government and Nazi Germany and fascist Italy intervened to help him while America and its allies refused aid. The Soviet Union aided the Republican side. To the Popular Front, a clearer battle of good versus evil did not exist. Unfortunately, a more in-depth knowledge of what happened in Spain would have shown the Communists opposed any form of revolution, worker or peasant unrest, or tampering with property rights. As George Orwell would show in his classic *Homage to Catalonia* (1952), the Communists, including the Soviet secret police, imprisoned and murdered thousands of radicals in the POUM (Workers' Party of Marxist Unification) because they were anarchists and Trotskyists unwilling to abide by the Stalinist leadership and demanded a socialist revolution, including taking over land and factories. Orwell's book would not come out for many years, but it likely would have been denied in any event by the quasi-religious supporters of the Soviet Union. Stalin and his followers consistently opposed revolution to uphold the bourgeois governments of the world.

- Regardless of issues, the Stalinists and their supporters were known for goon tactics in their actions in political and cultural fronts and in the labor movement where they gained an important entrée through the grace of John L. Lewis, who decided that he would hire Communists to help organize the CIO (Congress of Industrial Organizations) in the 1936–37 period. Roger Baldwin—founder and head of the American Civil Liberties Union and a major progressive supporter for most of the 1930s (he was the leader of a major Popular Front organization, the League Against War and Fascism [later changed to the League for Peace and Freedom])—later wrote of the party:

"They mislead unsuspicious liberals into their political traps. They pervert democratic procedures in many associations to achieve control by a minority. They are adept at concealing their identities; they hide behind false fronts. They have an irresistible lust for power." (Cottrell 2000, p. 310)

The Communist Party members were known for their vast knowledge of parliamentary procedure, commitment to work all hours and endure any barriers to the cause, and ability to caucus ahead of time to plan each move in an organization. This provided them power to control numerous organizations that they were neither a majority of nor had democratically been elected to. In many organizations, the average member lacks commitment to stay for long meetings and to prepare ahead of time to vote on obscure parliamentary issues and is too busy with their day jobs or responsibilities to give all their time to a cause.

But on top of skill, the party members did not often reveal themselves. On one level, this was understandable. To say, particularly in the blue-collar labor movement they were so prominent in, that you were a communist not only bred suspicion and sometimes anger but was also, in some cases, against the bylaws of the unions. Ottanelli (1991, p. 155) says these members were called "submarines" in the party vernacular. That is, they were secret party members, many of whom had achieved a high rank in union office or in political or social organizations. Former Communist Roy Hudson noted a big problem with concealing membership in the CP: "It breeds distrust among workers. They cannot understand why we are ashamed; why we hide the fact that we are Communists?" (ibid., p. 155). In some ways, the party had wounded itself, at least if the goal was to convert people to communism.

But the true goal of the Popular Front period was not that at all but, on the contrary, to gain power for the party itself and to presumably prevent fascism's success by getting the United States to ally with the Soviet Union. Unfortunately, the Communist tactics left a very bad taste in many people's mouths. Imagine you support John Jones as president of your union. He seems to be a good man. In his speeches, he supports the rights of labor and better conditions for workers. You do not know his personal politics, but he seems to be one of the guys. Imagine your surprise when after he wins as president, Jones refuses to support a wildcat strike because this would embarrass him and the union leadership (the CP in part because of their loyalty to the unions who tolerated them refused to be disloyal to them). Jones refuses to hold many open union meetings but has committee meetings at odd times and places. Then somehow, when the party line changes, so does Jones. He was a militant when he ran for office, but in the war years, he will be nearly right-wing (see below) and be against anything that reduces productivity. He becomes a bosses' man whom you really can't stand.

The bitterness that emerged in the late 1940s was not just plain anti-communism and McCarthyism alone. It was greatly aided by the hostility of rank-and-file workers (and others) who felt misused by the party and its supporters who conducted themselves in an undemocratic and manipulative way. Having seen the twists and turns of the party and the slavish devotion to the Soviet Union of its members and supporters, the average person was not impressed by what it understood as communism.

Why Did They Do It? Progressive Motivations

It is always hard to put oneself back in history. Certainly, major factors in the development of the popularity of the Communists and progressives for a few years were the Great Depression and the prestige of the Russian Revolution. For many people and, perhaps, particularly intellectuals and professionals who were aware of theoretical writing, the Great Depression seemed to be the gravedigger of capitalism. The worldwide collapse did not seem remediable by capitalist reform, and the world only needed some push to move to communism, many believed. The experiment in Russia had captured the imagination of many Americans since 1917, particularly intellectuals and some in labor. With capitalism collapsing, the Soviet Union seemed the clear choice of systems in the world. The Soviets were very good at propaganda and at covering up major problems. CP leader Dorothy Healey (1993, p. 61) speaks of how anyone who came back from the Soviet Union was "God incarnate, full of all the wisdom of the world." The Soviets took visitors to booming factories creating modern goods and to stalwart loyalists who praised Stalin; visitors seemed to not have seen the outlying areas where people suffered repression and loss of land or people who were sent to their deaths or imprisonment in the Gulags. Later, another Progressive (Henry Wallace, who would run on the Progressive Party platform in 1948) was caught in what was a major Soviet deception when he visited Siberia in 1944 and praised the city of Magda. It turned out Magda was a slave-labor city that had been "elaborately transformed into a 'Potemkin Village' prior to his visit" (Culver and Hyde 2001, pp. 330–339).

Further, no issue could solidity support than that of opposing fascism. On their own, support for the Soviet Union and even socialism was far more limited in America than the great shock of the rise of Hitler and Mussolini. Again, simple slogans of defeating fascism prevailed, and who could object? The CP appeal for unity against fascism combined with its strong stand on civil rights brought many Jews into the party orbit, and it also was successful with African-Americans for a time. Its claim to the democratic mantle and for peace, labor rights, and progressive legislation seemed unassailable and brought great prestige to the party for three or four years.

But not all the reasons for affiliation and support were selfless reasons. The party itself moved from being a proletarian existence to a respected middle-class operation. As Ottanelli quoted former CP member George Charney saying, "the proletarian garb favored by function-aries was replaced by the business suit; our professional revolutionaries could hardly be distinguished from office executives; bus travel was replaced by Pullman (rail cars); having children were no longer frowned upon, though hardly encour-aged; and the day Earl Browder (leader of the Communist Party) stood up in a restaurant to help his wife don her coat initiated a new standard of deportment." (Ottanelli 1991, p. 127)

Irving Howe places this embourgeoisement into a slightly broader context:

"It was exceedingly pleasant to be lead-ing a party that had opened an attractive headquarters, enjoyed good relations with local politicians and trade-union leaders, and could attract seven or eight thousand people to a rally ... they were able to reach [Congressman in Harlem] Adam Clayton Powell on the phone ... enrolled a bril-liant array of Harlem talent ... [they had] respectability, comfort, secretaries, good salaries, docile staff, admiring followers— all came together to soften and allure." (Howe 1985, pp. 100–101)

Of course, all this had an effect on the ideology of the Communists. Dorothy Healy shares some of this in her book (Healey and Isserman 1993, pp. 71–72), expressing how dazzled she was to have friends at the National Labor Relations Board (NLRB) and the Farm Security Administration (FSA) as well as in the state government of California. She no longer felt that state officials represented the capitalist class or had "sold out" or been "co-opted." Rather, she now felt it made a big difference who was in office. But naturally, this was the whole purpose of the New Deal and other liberal reforms: to show radicals there was a modicum of difference between parties and that if people accepted the restraints of capitalism, the officials would be happy to work with them. The party and progressives bought into liberal capitalism.

If the Communist Party members became more bourgeois, what can be said for the Popular Front progressives? Howe and Coser note how the big names were the stars the CP sought:

"All the party now cared about was that they be used as 'stars' in the elaborate network of front organizations, it wanted names, signatures, faces, 'prominent figures' … beneath an upper echelon … there milled about a horde of second rate intellectuals, Hollywood scripters, radio hacks, popular novelists, English professors, actors, dancers, newspapermen and publicity agents." (Howe and Coser 1962, p. 314)

Perhaps the best example of an ardent fellow traveler was Roger Baldwin of the American Civil Liberties Union and head of the largest Popular Front group, the League Against War and Fascism, from 1936 to 1939. Baldwin was from an affluent background who turned, for a while, into an anarchist enamored of Emma Goldman. Baldwin was a complex man and a radical in many ways, but according to his biographer, he was a man exceedingly subject to flattery and the appeal of power. On the one hand, Baldwin, though he did not join the party, was a stalwart loyalist to the Popular Front for some years. Some called him the archetype fellow traveler; and he and his friend J. B. Matthews, a linguist and educator, called themselves "united front twins" (Cottrell 2000, p. 217). Yet, as Cottrell notes, Baldwin always had a good relationship with the FDR administration and officials in government. He even came to like some key enemies like J. Edgar Hoover and, later, Gen. Douglas MacArthur. Baldwin's attitude was not from a Christian love-all place but from an egocentric desire to be liked by all sides, from the communists to the officials in government. Baldwin most reminds me of the radical chic days of the 1960s when composer Leonard Bernstein had the Black Panthers over for dinner. Not surprisingly, Cottrell found that Baldwin "had an amazingly unsophisticated reading of communist Russia … like many other Western intellectuals, he seemed to view the Soviet leaders as super progressives of a sort" (p. 176) and "at the time of the Moscow trials he believed the Soviets were achieving great accomplishments and was still the most democratic nation in the world" (p. 236). Interestingly, when Baldwin shifted his thinking by 1939, like many other former party supporters among progressives, he became an ardent foe of communism leading in red-baiting.

It is important though not to paint the progressive fellow travelers with one brush. Two leading figures in Popular Front organizations—A. Philip Randolph of the National Negro Congress and Joseph Lash of the student organizations that had several acronyms—came out well.

Randolph was a long-time member of the Socialist Party who had edited the radical paper the *Messenger* for years. The African-American leader, without relying on CP or others, was able to organize the Brotherhood of Sleeping Car Porters (BSCP)—the largest union of African-Americans at the time. After a long fight to secure recognition for the union, Randolph became a leading figure in the black community. He had already refused entreaties from many CP organizations (as a Socialist Party member, he had experienced firsthand the bitter attacks of the CP as early as the 1920s), but in the late 1930s, he did accept the presidency of the National Negro Congress. The NNC was a little different from some other front groups as it was an umbrella organization of a number of different groups. By the late 1930s, like many others, Randolph could not abide the Communist presence in the organization; and when the Hitler-Stalin Pact had begun to erode the CP strength, he resigned from his office. Randolph did not miss a beat in social change, showing how many actions were possible without the CP. Forming the March on Washington Movement (MOWM), he and some of his black allies from the Socialist Party who would also become household names in the 1960s, Bayard Rustin and James Farmer, believed the time had come to integrate the army. Randolph threatened FDR that he would draw 250,000 black bodies to line up in front of the White House. As Marian Berry tells the story (2018, chapter 1, see also Bynum 2010 and ANB 2000), Roosevelt was fearful and had his wife, Eleanor, and mayor of New York Fiorello La Guardia meet with Randolph, two progressives as well. Randolph called off the march in exchange for the formation of the Fair Employment Practices Committee, which would hear complaints of racial discrimination. After World War II, Randolph organized the movement to again threaten then president Harry Truman with a mass march. After a stand-off, Truman gave in and, after more than a century of segregation, did integrate the military. Randolph's historic advocacy of the march on Washington led to the famous 1963 civil rights march in Washington, DC, at which Martin Luther King gave his "I have a dream" speech.

Joseph Lash, a student at the City College of New York, helped build "the first mass student protest movement in American history" (ANB 2000). Lash, a Socialist Party member and a pacifist, led campaigns against war for many years in which students signed pledges not to fight. Amazingly for the times, Lash helped negotiate a merger between the Socialist Party–led Student League for Industrial Democracy (SLID) and the Communist Party–led National Student League (NSL) into the American Student Union (ASU). He served as the most influential leader of the new group. Like others, the Hitler-Stalin Pact of 1939 ended his ability to ally with the Communists in the Popular Front, and he resigned. Lash later became a well-known author and biographer of Eleanor Roosevelt and Helen Keller, among others.

The Hitler-Stalin Pact

One of the few things that all observers, communist, progressive, and anti-communist agree on is the shock the 1939 Hitler-Stalin Pact had on Americans. Many, like Roger Baldwin, called it a bombshell; and Communists, like Healey, kept checking mass media to make sure they were hearing correctly. Having judged the Soviet Union at risk, Stalin switched horses and negotiated a treaty with Nazi Germany, one which also allowed Russian troops to take part of Poland and later invade Finland as well. While justified by loyalist CPers as a protection for the Soviet Union, it broke up the Popular Front and caused many people to quit a variety of front organizations, including the Communist Party itself.

The Popular Front against fascism, as we have seen, was the central element of the CP's program and its raison d'être in attracting many new members in the 1930s.

When it was learned the Soviets were allying with Hitler, it sent pains throughout the progressive world.

Among the many progressives who would leave the CP orbit in 1939 were Roger Baldwin, Adolf Berle (a prominent attorney and FDR aide), Van Wyck Brooks (a nonfiction literary writer), writer Malcolm Cowley, actor Melvyn Douglas, attorney and (later) Supreme Court Justice Abe Fortas, writer Ernest Hemingway, poet Archibald MacLeish, writer Thomas Mann, inventor and scientist Lewis Mumford, minister Reinhold Niebuhr, and poet William Carlos Williams. All the major popular front organizations—the writers' league, the National Negro Congress, the American Student Union, and the National League for Peace and Democracy—were left in crumbles. How many members were lost is controversial, but it seems to have been in the thousands at least. Some also were in shock and, more quietly, left a little later.

The party, showing its ability to adjust to shifts and turns, attacked the warmongers in America and called for peace. Abandoning its earlier praise for preparedness, it now did everything to be pacifists, tending to—as ten years before—identify the capitalists of each country as being similar and not worth fighting for. Such rhetoric and slogans caused pain particularly among the progressives who had allied with the party.

World War II

The Nazi invasion of the Soviet Union in 1941 put an end to the Communist Party's isolation. Not missing a beat after two years of support for peace and declaring the imperialism of both the Axis and the Allies, the party and progressives now could join the war effort with the Soviets and Americans as partners in a Grand Alliance. The party was totally for the New Deal "as a way of progress, democracy and peace," and its slogan was "Unite the American people around the New Deal and its progressive policies" (Ottanelli 1991, pp. 180, 186).

The party would so much support the government that it looks quite extreme to future generations. In 1941, the US government indicted twenty-nine members of the Socialist Workers Party under the Smith Act against espionage and treason. Dorothy Healey, then a party member, shudders that "to our discredit not only did [we] refuse to come to their support but [we] actually organized to prevent other people from supporting them" (Healy and Isserman 1993, pp. 114–115). It did not take much of a crystal ball to see that the CP would itself become a victim of the Smith Act. They, too, would be indicted in 1948. But to the CP, the SWP were Trotskyists and hence ipso facto guilty of anything charged. The charges involved no overt acts but only written and oral words against the government.

A second tragedy was the failure of the CP (or hardly any progressives) to say anything about the internment of Japanese-American citizens in relocation camps. Healey notes that the party, which was large and active in California, knew quite a few of the Japanese people. But

> "so unquestioning was our support that we raised no objections when Japanese-American citizens ... were sent to reloca-tion camps. It is yet another example of our inability to find or conceive of a way to be simultaneously supportive and criti-cal in our judgements." (p. 86)

The party also was so gung ho for the military effort; it also was critical of African-Americans who were cam-paigning for a victory over Jim Crow in the war years to end segregation. The party labeled this effort as disrup-tive as it would "sabotage the war effort, aiding the Axis camp and endangering the unity of the American people" (cited in Howe and Coser 1962, pp. 415–16). It asked that African-Americans suspend their fight for rights until the war ended!

The party also ran into conflicts with the labor move-ment—some of which would cause its largest remaining base to desert them after the war years. The party not only embraced the no-strike pledge many unions took in the war but also enforced it on the rank and file more than others. The party denounced strikes as helping to lose the "battle of production." It said, "any strike is bound to prove a hindrance to the war effort." Business spokesmen were at first taken aback to discover that the Communists now stood at the extreme right wing of the labor movement. *Businessweek* noted that unions identified as Communist had "best no-strike record" (ibid., pp. 408–9). Additionally, and to the horror of the labor movement, the party sup-ported incentive pay that would produce a speedup for workers and a labor draft, opposed by the unions, that would have subjected workers to immediate drafts (see Healey and Isserman 1993, p. 92; Ottanelli 1991, p. 206).

Earl Browder, the long-time chair of the Communist Party, was so carried away by the spirit of the time. He declared that "we will not raise any socialist proposals for the United States in any form that can disturb national unity." A broader promise to make capitalism work was made in 1944:

"Marxists will not help the reactionaries by opposing the slogan of 'Free
Enterprise' with any form of counter-slo-
gan ... we are ready to cooperate in making Capitalism work effectively ... I would
get along fine with National Association
of Manufacturers." (cited in Howe and
Coser 1962, p. 427)

Browder began going too far when on the same year,
he proposed that even after the war, the Communist Party
would commit itself to class collaboration and unity with
all forces and would end the party, replacing it with a
Communist Political Association.

This was too much. Healey remembers hearing
about it only in an article in the *Los Angeles Times*. She
was shocked and in tears. In May 1945, Jacques Duclos, a
French Communist, writing in a party paper, condemned
Browder; and shortly after, Browder was axed as the US
Communist leader. According to Healey, a wave of tearful
confessions occurred within party circles in which people
said how wrong Browder was and how he was guilty of
revisionism. Howe and Coser note that even after fifteen
years in power and having about the best relationship with
Moscow, "Browder was powerless in relation to Moscow,

what Stalin could raise, Stalin could destroy" (1962, p. 438). Hence ended the extremely embarrassing love affair between the party and American capitalism.

The Cold War and the Progressive Party of 1948

It is difficult to date precisely the beginning of the Cold War. We now know from archives that the atomic bombing of Japan in 1945 scared Stalin deeply and led him to fear the US even more (Swanson 2013), helping provoke his plan to surround the Soviet Union with friendly border states to protect Russian soil. After all, the Soviets had faced two invasions from the West from Germany in the twentieth century. In March 1946, Winston Churchill gave his famous "iron curtain" speech. Still, for at least a couple of years, it was unclear how deep and thoroughgoing the US-Soviet rivalry would be.

In the US, the year 1946 was a turning point. After a year marked by strikes across the country by workers who had suffered from lowered wages and war conditions, the country moved not left but right. The congressional elections saw a big victory for conservatives, including the election of such red-baiters as Joseph McCarthy, senator from Wisconsin, and Richard Nixon, congressman from

California. The Congress quickly passed the Taft-Hartley Act, basically limiting many of the benefits of the Wagner Act. Anti-communist measures were well underway starting with Roger Baldwin and the ACLU. They had ironically led the way when they outlawed from any office "fascists, Nazis, and Communists"—a formulation quickly adopted by other groups. The ACLU board led by former fellow traveler Baldwin tried Elizabeth Gurley Flynn, an old IWW organizer who was an open CP member, expelling her. But the HUAC (House Un-American Activities Committee) hearings, begun in 1947, opened a new more vicious era of red-baiting with the calling of "friendly" witnesses who named names and "unfriendly witnesses," many of whom would later be indicted.

By 1946, the Communist Party, now under the leadership of its oldest comrade, William Z. Foster, became far more militant in its rhetoric (although there were no real implications for domestic policy). Foster warned the US was "on the road to fascism" and that "no other country [had] ever set for itself such all-inclusive imperial goals" (cited in Howe and Coser 1962, p. 455). However, as noted by Howe and Coser, all the party had built up in the labor unions over ten years was beginning to crumble. Joseph Curran of the National Maritime Union (NMU), once a CP ally, turned on them and used the party's collaborationist views in the war against them. Mike Quill of the Transport Workers Union (TWU), once known as "Red Mike" because of his Communist sympathies, would use every trick in the book "to tear up their [CP's] roots in American unions" (Howe and Coser 1962, p. 460).

Meanwhile, liberals, some of whom were once fellow traveling progressives, broke with the Communists and founded the ADA (Americans for Democratic Action) in early 1947. These included many famous names such as theologian Reinhold Niebuhr and autoworker chief Walter Reuther, both of whom had been allied with the left at times, as well as Hubert Humphrey (then mayor of Minneapolis), columnist Joseph Alsop, historian Arthur Schlesinger, economist John Kenneth Galbraith, and for-mer first lady Eleanor Roosevelt. Liberals firmly broke away from the CP progressive pole and took a strong anti-com-munist and anti-Soviet stand.

In what was becoming an extremely disconcerting environment, the Communist Party and progressives came up with a strategy: found a new Progressive Party. The plan to secure five million votes, had it worked, would indeed have at least somewhat limited President Harry Truman's plans to surround the Soviet Union; and of course, there was no certainty at all that Truman would win as he was nowhere close to FDR's popularity. The man for the job was Henry Wallace, vice president under FDR in 1941–45 and a former agriculture secretary and commerce secretary. On paper, Wallace, an Iowa farmer who became an agricultural expert, was strong. He was as American as apple pie. He reminded people of the New Deal and Midwestern progressivism.

Wallace, unfortunately, somewhat like fellow traveler Baldwin, was a paradoxical man who was tagged as a radical while really, in his own terms, a "progressive capitalist." But his statements were all over the place, sometimes confusing friends as well as enemies. A big New Deal fan, his rhetoric was dramatic:

> (On Jackson Day, 1944)" The New Deal is as old as the wants of man ... is Amos proclaiming the needs of the poor in the land of Israel. The New Deal is New England citizens dumping tea in Boston Harbor ... it is Andrew Jackson marching in the twentieth century... [it] is Abraham Lincoln preaching freedom for the oppressed. It is the New Freedom of Woodrow Wilson." (Culver and Hyde 2001, p. 321)

His friendship with the Soviets seemed genuine. Though, as noted by his tour when he was vice president, he was easily fooled and naive. He seemed to have honestly believed, as many progressives do today as well, that the "primary effort of progressives may be to rebuild the Democratic Party as a liberal party" (ibid., p. 433). Faced with a campaign that centered greatly on the Marshall Plan, a plan that evoked in many Americans the spirit that it was just helping out the poor Europeans devastated by war, he opposed it without clear reasons. He said, "I certainly do not want to see communism spread. I predict Truman's policy will spread communism in Europe and Asia" (ibid., p. 437). He eagerly believed that "capitalism and communism can resolve their conflicts without resort to war" (ibid., p. 440).

Having been a Democrat for so long and having worked for two presidents, he was particularly subject to attack on his politics and character. Truman claimed that he had met with Wallace, who had told him he was a pacifist and he "wanted to disband our armed forces" (ibid., p. 425). It was hard to disprove the combination of pacifism and pro-communism he was charged with. Although Wallace gained a fair number of famous endorsements— Helen Keller, Charlie Chaplin, Albert Einstein, Katharine Hepburn, Edward G. Robinson, John Garfield, and Hedy

Lamarr, for example—early polls that were favorable began to sink nearer to election time. As often the case, third parties face the "spoiler" charge particularly in a close election. Most fatally, the labor movement, once the heart of CP influence, was, as Healey notes, "moving closer to Truman." The combination of Truman's veto of Taft-Hartley, his adoption of a liberal program, and his anti-communism seemed to have influenced the rank and file. Additionally, as she points out, Wallace was not on the ballot everywhere, and he had no down-ticket supporters (Healey and Isserman 1993, pp. 110–111). Gallup noted that almost one-third of Wallace's supporters in October deserted as the election approached (Culver and Hyde 2001, p. 500).

Wallace ended up as the weakest of the three Progressive Party candidates, gaining only 1.1 million votes or 2.3 percent on the election. Only in New York, California, and Illinois did Wallace garner a significant number of votes. Truman, of course, squeezed out a narrow victory over liberal Republican Thomas Dewey, and the States' Rights Party carried about an equal number of votes as Wallace. The Progressive Party would have a short life span afterward, and Wallace himself began moving away from his earlier positions, supporting the US and UN troops when the war in Korea broke out in 1950.

The election, in retrospect, has to be seen as aiding the move to the right and the strengthening of McCarthyism in America. With such a narrow range of support, HUAC was freed to indict communists, the AFL-CIO threw out eleven unions as communist-dominated, and purges began in government—from the federal government to small school districts. McCarthyism destroyed many lives, some literally from suicide. The Communist Party was decimated by arrests, by others going underground, and by many despairing members leaving the party. *Progressive* also was a word not much heard for a while.

Nevertheless, it is important to remember that the anti-communist witch hunt had little or nothing to do with any radicalism in the CP. As we have seen, at least, in the 1936–1948 period, the party did no more than mouth liberal platitudes although its party members (only some, according to accounts by both Healey and Isserman and Howe and Coser) may have ever read Marx, Lenin, and Stalin. While the Communists praised democracy, their tactics were Stalinist and turned off potential supporters. McCarthyism was caused by a combination of the scary events in the world of the late 1940s and early 1950s in which the USA felt communism was going to win the world's support (particularly after the Communist Revolution in China in 1949) and opportunistic right-wing politicians who saw a great issue to win support and move away from the relative liberalism of fifteen years before.

Unfortunately, there has been relatively little discussion on the left of the Communist Party. When the New Left arose in the early 1960s, it wisely rejected the anti-communism of their elders. However, they did not learn any lessons from history either. Once again, while activists read Marx and Lenin and Mao and sometimes Trotsky and Stalin, they did not read about the history of the American Left and proceeded to make familiar mistakes in many ways. It was unfortunately part of the widespread anti-intellectualism of the New Left that the past made no difference.

Takeaways: Continuity and Change

The 1930s and 1940s' record of progressives shows the continuity of this ideology and label from the first Progressive movement. Like the first movement, the major figures of the era (one can think not only of Roger Baldwin and Henry Wallace but also the long list of Popular Front supporters) were middle class in nature and supported reform, not revolution. Progressives approved of top-down politics. This took place in the many front organizations as well as unions, clubs, fraternal organizations, and other ordinary American groups. Rather than support a democratic movement, the progressives and the CP hid their political beliefs and worked with their supporters to take over these groups by working around democracy. The other form of politics to be entertained was electoral, supporting FDR for many years and then the Progressive Party candidacy. Like the earlier progressives, the leading figures were optimistic and naive, believing that people would easily forgive their missteps and that people were loyal to a liberalistic set of policies.

There was some change in the 1930s and 1940s. The main one was that the progressives, as a group and a label, had moved to the left. The position of progressives in the 1910s was far more ambiguous; after all, it was a party of Theodore Roosevelt and was later claimed as well by Woodrow Wilson. La Follette had (it is true) allied with the Socialist Party in 1924, but it was a one-shot affair and was opposed by many other progressives. However, the position of progressives as allies of the Communists left a more permanent imprint. On the one hand, the repression of communism diminished greatly the use even of the word. But when *progressive* came back as a term in the last several decades of the twentieth century and the first decades of the twenty-first century, it tended (though not universally) to be allied with the left. As one example, progressive candidacies of Jesse Jackson (1984 and 1988), Ralph Nader (multiple times in the twenty-first century), and Bernie Sanders (2016 and 2020), although they have differences, were all clearly on the left. The *Nation* and *New Republic* magazines, for example, provide a historical continuity between some of the 1930s left and today's. Progressives assiduously do not talk of their history as constant fellow travelers of both the Democratic Party and, at one point, the Communist Party.[6]

One unfortunate development from this has been a heightening of heated and simplistic rhetoric. Howe and Coser (1962, pp. 455–456) wisely note how the CP of the mid-1940s turned to simplistic rhetoric:

> "The Communists had to cry fascism: politically in order to justify extreme hostility to every aspect of foreign policy … Among Communist militants who remained in the party in the late forties and early fifties, the belief that fascism was close at hand constituted more than a theory: it quickly became part of a pervasive political mood … their crude simplifications … led to a style of propaganda frequently bordering on the hysterical."

This rhetoric has remained with us today, a residue of many decades of left-wing isolation and internal and external attacks. Today the calling of someone a fascist is a regular occurrence, whether the progressives are attacking President Trump, Democratic activists who do not fight him enough, or only those in different parts of the left whom people disagree with. Added to this is the frequent description of people and parties as racist often without any particular proof. While, of course, not one party bears the responsibility for the state of American politics and its discourse, it is unfortunate that progressives often play a major role in the debasement of public debate and the substitution of buzzwords instead.

FOUR

Progressives III: The Rapid Decline of Liberalism and Progressive as a New Name

"Why don't we call it (liberalism) progressive? It means looking to move and improve. It means family and pragmatism. So, progressive pragmatism. And it frees me of all the stereotypes. 'Liberal' brings all kinds of baggage."

—Mario Cuomo,
The New York Times (February 9, 1984)

This chapter will review how liberalism collapsed as a popular ideology from the late 1960s through the 1970s and 1980s and, in fact, became a term of derision not only among the radical left and the conservatives but also among many "disappointed liberals" themselves, as Edmund Fawcett terms them (2018, p. 379). These disappointed liberals were particularly those blue-collar workers and others among the poor and middle class whose parents had voted for FDR and Truman or had themselves once voted for Kennedy and Johnson. The Democratic Party itself, weakened by the rise of the New Right, veered to the right. As the years went on though, most liberals sought to bury the term *liberalism* and replace it with *progressivism*. Although many political candidates and officeholders use the term, the most continued and repeated usage of it was by those on the left-to-liberal side of the political spectrum who ran with the loosely defined term. Whether such candidates as Jesse Jackson or Ralph Nader actually acted in good faith in claiming to be a progressive or even radical rather than liberal is open to question.

Liberalism's Collapse

As an ideology, liberalism was always based on a series of paradoxes that would threaten its longevity. Although the Democratic Party was not the sole source of liberalism, which, to an extent, dominated the GOP as well,[2] it is easier to look at the contradictions on the Democratic side. It was a pro-capitalist party, like the Republicans, yet its voice for reform and sometimes its soaring rhetoric led some followers to forget that. It was never a labor party, unlike most Western countries had, where the dominant worker parties and trade unions held formal power; but the AFL-CIO, with some exceptions, was a strong backer of liberalism, particularly social welfare and labor legislation. It was a party of segregation in the South supporting Jim Crow laws, yet in the North, it contained many liberal white and African-American supporters who, already at mid-century, were aiming to break the Southern system. And while they warned of Republican warmakers, in actuality, as H. W. Brands (2001) well notes, it was the party of the Cold War. It was Harry Truman who built up to war state (opposed by some conservatives like Robert Taft), and when Eisenhower took over, he was deeply ambivalent and eventually warned of the dangers of the military-industrial complex. Again, Kennedy and Johnson proudly continued the Cold War and its associated hot wars. All these issues were going to lead to a collision at some point, and it did in the 1960s.

The collapse greatly occurred between Lyndon Johnson's landslide victory over conservative Barry Goldwater in 1964 and the highly charged 1968 electoral campaign that included the bloody battle at the Chicago Convention between police and protesters and ended with the election of Republican Richard Nixon over Democrat Hubert Humphrey (a noted Cold War liberal) and racist third-party candidate George Wallace of Alabama. The two most obvious catalysts of the crisis of liberalism were the Vietnam War and the aftermath of the Civil Rights Act, particularly the move of the battle for civil rights to the North.

It is important to view these and other issues that split the Democratic Party not only as some sort of rational issue selection but also symbolically by looking sociologically at which social classes and sectors of the population led the movements against the war and for civil rights in the North. In both cases, the growing anti-war movement of the mid-1960s and the more militant civil rights movement of the mid to late 1960s with advocates of Black Power, New Left students, and judicial activists who carried out lawsuits frightened and angered white working-class people. They saw those students and activists as people above them in social class and education, tearing down what they believed in (and had been told for years to believe in). Of course, the African-American movement included many people lower in the class structure; but a combination of racism, classism toward the poor, and working-class hostility to the experts who frequently were in the leadership combined to reinforce hostility. Many accounts of this class split have been written—Sennett and Cobb (1973) being a classic and David Croteau's (1995) book being a good application of social class to politics.

Having been a youth committed to both the anti-war movement and the civil rights struggle as well, it took me many years to see my activism as a function not only of my commitment but also of how it included aspects of privilege. As a student at Columbia University, I was buttressed from the risks that many activists take. After the 1968 campus takeovers, the university administration was loath for many years to call the police (also being at the foot of Harlem) even when students and others broke glass, threw rocks, or set fires. By my sophomore year, the lottery had come to replace the earlier draft system, and I had a fortunately high number. While our location at Columbia put us in contact with many militant African-Americans in Harlem, it did not place us in much contact with less militant African-Americans, working-class or poor white people, or those of other races and ethnicities except Puerto Ricans. Only when I experienced political contact in other parts of Manhattan and the other boroughs of New York City did I encounter pro-war citizens as well as those who disdained civil rights or at least saw civil rights as applying only to the South.

Had history been otherwise, both key movements might have been different. If the anti-war movement began not on campus but in the military, for example, it would have been a much more powerful and probably more sympathetic movement to the general population. Had leaders such as Martin Luther King been alive to steer the late 1960s movement, perhaps the stunning (to many white people) nature of the emergence of Black Power, along with groups like the Black Panthers and Black Muslims, would not have been so significant. Many point out that before his death, King was organizing the Poor People's Campaign to unite whites and people of color around economic issues. However, I tend to doubt the latter possibility would have changed the racial split. The ghetto riots and rise of crime in the 1960s profoundly affected the nation's attitude toward both the poor and the African-American people, and the tremendous appeal of "black is beautiful" and black nationalism (if not radicalism) was already widespread even while King was alive.[8] Unfortunately, as the New Left and other '60s movements ignored at their peril, a political rupture and backlash was inevitable and would last for many decades.

It is perhaps obvious to say that attitudes toward these movements spilled heavily over to almost every issue. As someone who has spent much of my life working with poor people and attempting to advocate for benefits for poor people, the disdain that emerged from the 1960s about "welfare queens" or "welfare cheats" or people living "off the system" has not gone into retreat even today despite the fact that the majority of poor people are white. It is still easier for people to believe that both recipients of benefits and advocates are seeking to put one over on them, the highly taxed citizenry, than to imagine that they themselves might need benefits. It is hard to find an issue—capital punishment, crime and prisons, or even environmental issues—that is not affected by the 1960s conflicts.[2]

Neither right nor left nor center find fault in their positions in this controversial period, but they should. To take only one example, who came up with the idea of busing young schoolchildren from one usually working-class or poor neighborhood to another? As some critics have pointed out, the upper and upper middle classes were not affected by busing. And busing or no busing, by the 1980s, school segregation was greatly reinforced in most of the nation by whites pulling their children out of public schools to private and parochial schools. It is not easy to get an answer; but why weren't communities consulted for their ideas, why were voluntary moves not entertained, and why were new school building not entertained? The rushed policy decisions despite their good intent did not end well.

In any event, it became clear shortly after the 1968 election that this was not a one-shot-deal loss from liberalism. The amazingly one-sided election in 1972 between the rather charismatically challenged Richard Nixon and his openly liberal opponent George McGovern was crushing. McGovern won only in Massachusetts and in DC. 1972 marked the last year, as I write, that the Democratic Party has nominated an admitted liberal to a presidential candidacy. Whether the tagging of the McGovern candidacy as "triple A for acid, amnesty, and abortion" (Brands 2001, p. 131) was appropriate or not, it is certain that the vast majority of the electorate had little use for anti-war and student protesters, African-American militants, proponents of feminism and gay rights, and hippies. Moreover, Nixon was a smart president: he moved to the left to outflank the Democratic Party with a proposal for a guaranteed income, and his administration saw the signing of many new progressive pieces of legislation for the environment, workers' safety, and indexing of Social Security to inflation and even opened the diplomatic relations with China. This was not to mention ending, albeit in a painfully slow way, the Vietnam War. Had it not been for the Watergate scandal, Nixon may have led to a continued period of moderate to liberal Republicanism.

Nothing among the many years between the McGovern candidacy and the era of Barack Obama augured well for the Democrats and liberals. In 1976, various liberals like Fred Harris of Oklahoma and Mo Udall of Arizona ran for president, but they were easily defeated by Jimmy Carter with his clean-cut outsider image, but centrist politics. By 1979, tired of Carter's failing presidency, noted liberal Edward Kennedy of Massachusetts ran to replace him as the party's nominee and lost. In turn, Carter was handily defeated by conservative Ronald Reagan, and liberal-leaning Walter Mondale was, in turn, defeated for Reagan's second term in 1984. Even with the tide of the new name *progressive*, a technocratic Mike Dukakis of Massachusetts won the nomination over more liberal Jesse Jackson and others like Paul Simon of Illinois in 1988 only then to lose to Republican George H. W. Bush. Finally, the New Democrat Bill Clinton, who openly broke with the tenets of liberalism, won back the presidency in 1992 and 1996 for the Democrats. Still, running as a centrist in 2000, Al Gore lost the contested election to George W. Bush; and in 2004, John Kerry, beating the more liberal John Edwards and Howard Dean (both of whom had self-destructed), also lost to Bush.

Putting aside for the moment where to classify Barack Obama, for at least forty years, the Democratic Party failed to place a liberal in the White House and, of course, in many state capitals and House and Senate seats as well. The time to use *liberal* as a descriptor seemed over for many activists in the party.

Moving to the Right: The New Right and the Centrist DLC

Not surprisingly, the key political takeaway of the 1970s onward was a sharp move to the political right. To the surprise of both parties, the New Right emerged powerfully in the 1970s aided by religious fundamentalism, direct-mail genius, and plenty of money. The New Right's politics were anti-1960s—for school prayer, the right to life, anti-feminism, antigay rights, a powerful military, return to basics in education, and so on. It found its hero in Ronald Reagan even though Reagan was more loyal to his anti-communist foreign policy and his supply-side economics, and arguably, he did not do too much for his social conservative supporters.

Meanwhile, the Democrats—who, with Carter, had already turned to the center—moved further right as well. In 1984, the *New York Times* writer Warren Weaver Jr. contrasted the platform passed by the National Convention with the 1976 one. Changes included deleting any reference to school busing as a remedy for segregation; excluding almost all references to welfare and anti-poverty programs; for the first time, speaking with disapproval that there were "25 million regular abusers of marijuana in the country" (in the 1970s, marijuana legalization seemed near); and condemning the Soviet threat, weakening its earlier platforms for nuclear arms control and peace (Weaver 1984). Only on the issues of abortion rights and homosexual rights (the latter nowhere near the full rights accorded more than twenty-five years later) were moves to the right not seen.

The Democratic Leadership Council (DLC) was founded the very next year. It was created by a number of centrist Democratic politicians like Al Gore (Tennessee), Sam Nunn (Georgia), Dick Gephardt (Missouri), Bruce Babbitt (Arizona), and Lawton Chiles (Florida). The DLC frankly urged an abandonment of liberalism and populism to go a third way. Popularized by the DLC's Bill Clinton and in the United Kingdom by Tony Blair, the third way was never a clear way as it only indicated it was different from communism and laissez-faire liberalism. It preferred complex technocratic strategies (such as Clinton's crazy-quilt health plan, which was defeated in 1993) to more government spending. It was socially liberal in some areas (such as women's rights) but tough on the dividing issues of the past (crime, the death penalty, welfare, the drug war, and so on), making sure to condemn prior liberalism.

Bill Clinton's administration confirmed all the worst fears of liberals. He made sure to return to his home state of Arkansas in early 1993 to preside over the execution of a mentally retarded man to show his support of the death penalty. He promoted the Crime Bill of 1994 to put more cops on the street and to increase penalties for drugs, leading to more incarceration, proving the Democrats were not soft on crime. In 1996, President Clinton signed the Personal Responsibility Act or welfare reform, ending, as he said, "welfare as we know it." Many people were cut off the welfare rolls, time limits were imposed on "welfare," and many people became ineligible. Somewhat less dramatically, the administration helped rein in government spending, following up on the President Clinton's declaration that "the era of big government is over." Democrats had joined Reagan's call against government.

Why Progressive? The Popularity of Vagueness

As the quote at the frontpiece above from New York's governor and one of America's leading liberals Mario Cuomo suggests, the name *progressive* was popular because it could mean whatever one wanted. A 1985 the *New York Times*/CBS News poll found that of all the major labels—conservative, moderate, liberal, populist, etc.—progressive ran the best numbers. The poll showed, for example, that *liberal* was quite contested with only 15 percent voicing support and 17 percent opposing (this obscured big regional differences such as in the South where 26 percent disapproved of liberalism). *Populist* failed as a substitute, receiving only 6 percent support and 21 percent opposition. But *progressive* was popular with 37 percent approval, while only 7 percent opposed. The cynicism of politicians was evident in the article (Clymer 1985). Roger Stone, the Republican consultant, noted the conservative Jack Kemp called himself a progressive on occasion despite being conservative and said as follows:

> "Who among the voters is against progress," Mr. Stone mused, although he observed that "progress is in the eyes of the beholder, and some people would think it was progress to repeal the income tax, while others would think it was progress to increase it." (Clymer 1985)

Similarly, Ann Lewis of the liberal Americans for Democratic Action "reached cheerfully for progressive," but she said its meaning was clear. "Everyone knows it means 'pragmatic liberal'" (Clymer 1985).

The *New York Times* itself seemed to be skeptical of the word at times and used it only in conjunction with an individual calling themselves this or in conjunction with *liberal*. In one of the first articles mentioning progressives, back in 1978 when Tom Hayden—once a 1960s radical, but now a Democratic activist—and others met for a ten-year 1960 reunion, the *Times* wrote this:

> "Then, he and they were radicals. Now, those survivors of the civil rights and peace movements who are still seeking change, a small distillate of the throngs involved in direct action campaigns decade ago, call themselves progressives "'without a tinge of embarrassment.'" (Herbers 1978)

Frequently, *Times* writers noted the word as a personal preference. In a 1988 article about politician Mark Green, they noted, "Mr. Green prefers to call them [liberal groups] progressive." (Rosenthal 1988). In a 1996 article about FAIR (Fairness and Accuracy in Reporting), the reporter pressed Steve Rendell, a senior analyst for the group, for his beliefs.

> "Trying to pin him down on his own politics is unsatisfying. Is he a liberal?" 'I would call myself a progressive,' he says. 'Isn't that the same as a liberal?' 'If I had to define myself, I'd use the term 'progressive,'" he insists. (Hays 1996)

Adding to the confusion was the creation in 1989 of the Clintonesque Progressive Policy Institute (PPI), provided, among other things, another propaganda center not for a leftist or liberal progressive but for the pragmatic centrist progressivism.

Despite the vagueness and differences, in terms of our book, what is clear is that those who were on the so-called political left immediately adopted the term and were the only group to use it not as an individual label but as a movement label. For this reason, I will focus this chapter's discussion on two political movements that declared themselves as progressive: the Jesse Jackson campaigns for the Democratic nomination for the presidency in 1984 and 1988 and the Ralph Nader campaigns as an independent or Green candidate for the presidency in the first decade of the 2000s. But it should be recognized that both uses of the term are out there as the 2020s begin. It is used as descriptive word by many politicians particularly in the Democratic Party, but it is used as righteous cause and label by left-of-center movements such as the campaigns of Sanders and Warren.

Jesse Jackson: Not Radical but Liberal

It is interesting how little it takes to be labeled a radical by the major media and the dominant parties. It seems anyone who challenges the leading politicians gets this label. Jesse Jackson, an African-American activist whose career with Operation Breadbasket (part of Southern Christian Leadership Conference or SCLC) and then with PUSH (People United to Save Humanity) were both marked by charges of financial irregularities, was hardly radical, but he rather had reformist efforts to increase the number of African-American employees in some businesses and to increase the number of black capitalists. In the spectrum of the civil rights and African-American movement, he hardly would be outside of the center-liberal arena. Evidentially, the combination of Jackson's soaring rhetoric, his willingness to visit and hug Fidel Castro and Yasser Arafat, and his efforts beginning in the 1980s to support labor strikes led him to be called a radical. Similarly, consumer advocate and activist Ralph Nader—famous for his *Unsafe at Any Speed* book and successful charges against the auto industry, as well as his many consumer organizations such as PIRG (Public Interest Research Group)—was also hardly regarded as a leftist or radical. In fact, Paul Krugman quipped in the *New York Times*, "While fashionable radicals were preaching revolution; he was demanding safer cars" (Krugman 2000). To his credit, Nader was willing to move away from the two dominant capitalist parties and run as an independent. Like Jackson's campaigns within the Democratic Party, he adopted the term *progressive* and, as we shall see, adopted a progressive program. While both were critical of the Reagan and Bush administrations—and Nader also of Clinton and Gore—neither called for a break with capitalism, the two-party system, or the entire structure of American world dominance, really only taking on the missing role of liberals in the elections of the 1980s and 2000s.

This is not at all to diminish the credit due to Jackson for his 1988 campaign, which surprised many people. In 1984, his run for the presidential nomination was viewed as a black-protest campaign and was weakened by a variety of revelations such as his "Hymietown" comments about Jews and New York City and then his refusal to denounce the Rev. Louis Farrakhan for his anti-Semitic and pro-Hitler comments. While he won 3.2 million votes in the 1984 primaries, they were almost entirely from African-American voters (Dionne 1988). In contrast, running in his Rainbow Coalition strategy in 1988, Jackson courted votes from all and won 6.9 million votes and won eleven contests, seven primaries (Alabama, the District of Columbia, Georgia, Louisiana, Mississippi, Puerto Rico, and Virginia), and four caucuses (Delaware, Michigan, South Carolina, and Vermont). Nevertheless, his main base (about two-thirds of his vote) came from African-Americans. Interestingly, while the Rainbow Coalition had promised a coalition "of blacks, of the poor, of women, of homosexuals, of the unemployed" (Jakoubek 2005, p. 2), in fact, Jackson's white vote support occurred mostly among college and graduate school graduates, not the poor or unemployed (Dionne 1988).

In fact, a look at Jackson's campaign and issues discussed suggests little effort around most of the Rainbow. Other than his work with labor, often speaking with its leadership and sometimes striking workers, there was little outreach to poor and unemployed workers, to women, or to gays. If Jackson made major efforts to recruit these groups as well as other people of color—such as Latino/Hispanic, Asian-American, and Native Americans—it was not publicized. As is often the case with progressives, there was a top-down strategy often based on a fantasy of saying something is so when it is not, as if this would make it so.

Looked out with benefit of hindsight, Jackson's program seems anything but radical and often unrelated to some of the Rainbow groups. Wikipedia (https://en.wikipedia.org/wiki/Jesse Jackson) cited thirteen campaign platforms, and of these, most were not reported to have been even raised on the campaign trail:

- creating a Works Progress Administration–style program to rebuild America's infrastructure and provide jobs to all Americans
- reprioritizing the war on drugs to focus less on mandatory minimum sentences for drug users and more on harsher punishments for money-laundering bankers and others who are part of the supply end of supply and demand
- reversing Reaganomics-inspired tax cuts for the richest ten percent of Americans and using the money to finance social welfare programs
- cutting the budget of the Department of Defense by as much as 15 percent over the course of his administration
- declaring apartheid-era South Africa to be a rogue nation

- instituting an immediate <u>nuclear freeze</u> and beginning <u>disarmament</u> negotiations with the <u>Soviet Union</u>
- giving reparations to descendants of black slaves
- supporting family farmers by reviving many of <u>Roosevelt's</u> <u>New Deal</u>–era farm programs
- creating a single-payer system of <u>universal health care</u>
- ratifying the Equal Rights Amendment
- increasing federal funding for lower-level <u>public education</u> and providing free <u>community college</u> to all
- supporting the formation of a <u>Palestinian state</u>
- applying stricter enforcement of the <u>Voting Rights Act</u>

Most of these issues were standard liberal fare, not that different from those raised by other liberals in the race—for example, Michael Dukakis. The Democrats clearly argued for an end to Reaganomics and to restore some amount to domestic programs; favored measures to end apartheid; supported family farmers; ratified the ERA (which Republican presidents Nixon and Ford also favored); increased aid to education; more strictly enforced the Voting Rights Act, a nuclear freeze, and a lessening of the drug war; and so forth. In fact, Jackson's moderation is evident in his drug-war views. While many were already calling for an end to the war and legalizing at least certain drugs, Jackson refused to consider legalization even of marijuana (Rosenthal 1988). Further, his answer to unemployment is not merely liberal but also pretty unimaginative (reviving a Works Progress Administration) at a time when labor and leftists were talking about shortening the work week to provide more jobs and creation of new industries and higher living wages. Although his figure of cutting the Defense budget was probably higher than any of his fellow candidates, it does not deal systemically with the problems of US foreign policy and also how to move military personnel to areas where they could be employed.

The only three proposals that some might consider radical might be the Palestinian state, the single-payer health care, and the reparations for slavery. But more and more liberal Democratic activists would support these over time, and none of them break with the liberal paradigm. Much of the world had already backed a two-state solution to the Middle East with Israel and a Palestinian state, the same as Jackson presumably backed. The single-payer health care is another magic word for some of the left and liberals. First, almost all countries in the world have a government health program, so the proposal is not radical. But second, as with other candidates such as Nader (see below) and Sanders (see below), little attention is paid to how the dominant private health-care companies and industries could be put out of business in the United States, where they are entrenched and make up some of the most profitable industries of the nation. Somehow, simply declaring for a universal or single-payer health system is meant to signal something, but it gives no idea of how this will create affordable, low-cost health care. None of these candidates has been actually willing to confront the major problems of health care, which is the most expensive of any nation in the world by far. The issue of reparations for slavery was not much discussed in the campaign and, while perhaps radical to some, was too ill-defined to make much comment. How would the nation identify those who were descendants of slaves as opposed to others? Would years of slavery be investigated and chronicled? What about free blacks and those who escaped slavery? It may be that reparations would be extremely divisive. And while arguably just, how much money would be devoted to the issue? If the amount was small, it would be bound to make recipients angry and unappreciative of the gesture. Getting away from pragmatics, his issues appear to be aimed at rallying certain supporters and not getting to the heart of issues as a radical would promise.

In addition to the symbolic nature of the reforms, for the most part, the platform never mentions gays at all, includes women only in regard to the ERA (not even equal pay or comparable worth), and says nothing of the needs of other people of color (reparations for Native Americans would seem an idea). Nor, except in a general way, is there any assistance or demands for the poor and unemployed—not even minimal calls for expanded benefits or replacement of welfare with a guaranteed income, for example.

Is he on the left? Sometimes yes, sometimes no. In an April 7, 1988, the *New York Times* article (Dowd 1988), he argued he was a centrist:

> "He [Jackson] compares his stances with those of Henry A. Kissinger and George P. Shultz, and he refers to the gray eminences of the establishment he recently had breakfast with in Washington, Clark M. Clifford and Clifford Alexander, as his policy advisers. He shrugged off the idea that some of his left-wing constituencies might have a hard time envisioning him in this new, more conservative mien, 'The center has shifted to include more people,' he said. "(Dowd 1988)

Jackson's rhetoric often denied that he was on the left at all. In his speech to the Democratic convention in July 1988 in summarizing first how each group needed the other (whites and blacks, gays and straights, men and women, etc.), he stated this:

> "Conservatives and progressives, when you fight for what you believe, right wing, left wing, hawk, dove, you are right from your point of view, but your point of view is not enough." (quoted in Gregory 2018, p. 93)

Jackson, the speechmaker, prized his role as peacemaker of the Democratic Party by then and hence was more interested in harmony and unity than any ideology. But this is the point: "what did Jesse want?" as many had asked in both 1984 and 1988, and the answer to this does not seem clear—whether ego satisfaction, the enormous attention he received, or actual concern for specific issues.

To observers at the *New York Times,* his 1988 campaign had earned him a cooperative and moderate political stripe. In March, Texas Democratic Party chairman Bob Slagle declared that Jackson was now an obedient Democrat:

"'I think everybody a year ago thought Jackson would be destructive,' Mr. Slagle said. 'Now Jackson has said enough times over that he's committed to the Democratic Party and its ultimate nominee that people have quit worrying about it.'"

A little more than a month later after a bruising New York primary in which Mayor Ed Koch lashed out at Jackson repeatedly in support of Albert Gore, the *New York Times* editorial board gave Jackson a blessing entitled "What Jesse Jackson Has Won."

"Nothing better symbolized Jesse Jackson's New York campaign, or confirmed the distance he has come since 1984, than the way he ended it. He told his supporters: 'We must have healing, we must have hope.' Then, without bitterness, he congratulated Michael Dukakis for a campaign that was 'credible and decent, with dignity above the fray.'"

Still, Jesse Jackson had accumulated the second highest number of delegates to front-runner Michael Dukakis, over 1,000 by convention time. What did Jesse want? The vice presidency? A cabinet position? Or as one article suggested (Oreskes 1988), "nudging the Democrats to [the] Left"? The article was so vague, as we have suggested already, to elude specifics. Oreskes noted maybe "he would press Mr. Dukakis for commitments for expanded domestic spending, tougher action against South Africa and other issues." Yet Oreskes could be specific about only a recently announced position paper by Jackson on expanding childcare. In fact, Oreskes noted the following:

> "While Mr. Dukakis's campaign leaders are practically gloating that they have gotten this far without making many detailed commitments that might hamper them in the fall election, Mr. Jackson's campaign sees this same point as a failing."

But while the media speculated about Jesse Jackson for three months, in the end, he, of course, did not get either the vice presidency, which went to conservative Lloyd Bentsen of Texas, nor did he get any platform changes that we know of. Biographer Robert Jakoubek asks the rhetorical question, "What did he [Jackson] get for giving a harmonious convention?" His answer is "Precious little!" Jackson did get his own private plane to campaign in, but not much else. Civil rights leader Hosea Williams was quoted saying, "Basically [Michael] Dukakis got Jesse [Jackson] in that meeting and told Jesse to go to hell," referring to a highly reported near convention meeting between the two men (Jakoubek 2005, pp. 10–11).

And so Jackson got his plane and campaigned diligently for Dukakis and Bentsen, whom he had earlier called a sop to the party's conservative wing (Ratcliffe 1988; Madigan and Tackett 1988). As we know, despite resisting liberal party platforms, Dukakis was easily defeated in November 1988 by George H. W. Bush, who capitalized on Dukakis's own liberalism by charging he was a card-carrying member of the ACLU and by using Dukakis's release, as governor of Massachusetts, of a black felon named Willie Horton over and over again in campaign ads to show that Dukakis was soft on crime.

And what became of Jackson? He became, as Oreskes predicted, a senior party statesman. He supported Bush's first Gulf War, Operation Desert Shield, in 1991; and despite condemning Clinton's DLC as the "Democratic Leisure Class," he came to endorse Clinton (Jakoubek 2005, pp. 107, 110). Bill was appreciative: "When Jesse decided to support me, he went all the way, with a barn burner [speech] that brought the house down" (ibid., p. 111). So much for another progressive-liberal effort.

Nader Tries Progressivism outside the Two Parties

In at least one way, Ralph Nader broke with the progressive mold of most of the progressive activists of the twentieth century (except for the brief excursions of Roosevelt, La Follette, and Wallace into the various Progressive parties) and ran as an independent. His doing so, most famously in 2000 when he was bitterly charged with being a spoiler who prevented Democratic candidate Albert Gore from winning the election (this issue is still very contested among experts), but again in 2004 and 2008, led to extreme hostility from the Democrats and much of its allied liberal activists. In 2000, Nader ran with the backing of the Green Party, and in the other elections, as an independent.

Despite this difference, an analysis of his campaigns, including his campaign issues and his lack of interest in creating a competing entity to the two major parties, seem, to me, to place him in the same category of progressives-qua-liberals who have diligently but quite unsuccessfully fought the dominant political machines. To an even greater degree than the Jackson campaign, Nader's issues are hard to pin down partly because the media tended to ignore them to focus solely on the horse race aspect of the campaign and on the constant discussion of his spoiler role. Additionally, though perhaps because Nader did not expect to win (he had hoped to gain 5 percent of the vote in 2000), he did not enunciate many of his ideas in detail. Nader did speak to large crowds of over ten thousand in quite a few cities—Austin (Texas), Boston, Chicago, Los Angeles, New York, Oakland (California), Seattle, and others. And he gained the support of many famous stars such as filmmaker Michael Moore, actors Susan Sarandon and Tim Robbins, comedian/actor Bill Murray, singers Ani DiFranco and Patti Smith, and former television host Phil Donahue. The following issues or proposals were gleaned:

- universal, single-payer health care (he specified the Canadian system at one point)
- significant cuts in military spending
- a major increase in minimum wage and securing of a living wage
- public financing of election campaigns
- doing away with the NAFTA (North American Free Trade Agreement)
- ending corporate welfare, of which many examples were given

- changing the labor laws to improve the ability of people to form unions
- major reform in the criminal justice system and opposition to death penalty and the Crime Bill
- going against the drug war and supporting legalization of marijuana
- improving mass transit

In some ways, because Nader focused on corporate power and crime than Jackson, his campaign issues were a little more unified and coherent than Jackson's. And indeed, he had taken flak for refusing to spend a large amount of time on identity politics. When he ran in 2000, he was immediately criticized by the *Nation* columnist Katha Pollitt for having "focused too much on trade issues, to the exclusion of matters like race relations, health care, and gay and abortion rights" (Dao 2000). While Nader certainly did give a focus on health care, his support for gay rights and civil rights and abortion (right to choose) were not highlighted as much.

But as discussed with Jackson above, my main comments are the reliance on the dominant liberal discourse for Nader's issues and the sort of naivete of progressivism. In a site called Ralph Nader on the Issues, for example, Nader is quoted as having made the following statements about foreign policy:

- US should be the world's humanitarian super-power. (Feb 2008)
- Corporate activity destroys the third world. (Jul 2004)
- Redefine national purpose to solve Third World scourges. (Jun 2000)
- Support foreign peasants instead of foreign dictators. (Jun 2000)
- Support social and economic justice across the globe. (Jun 2000)
- Assist Russia & Israel in moving towards better governments. (Jun 2000)
- Selling arms is not a good way to conduct foreign affairs. (Feb 2000)
- Cuba: corporate sales of junk undermines their system. (Feb 2000)
- Support human rights as cornerstone of US foreign policy. (Jun 2000)

Although most of these comments seem to be so vague as to be unobjectionable, but how is a government that is charged by Nader and other progressives with dominating the world and helping maintain a US and capitalist impe-rialism going to suddenly shift to "supporting foreign peas-ants instead of foreign dictators" and being the "world's humanitarian superpower"? These thoughts may sound nice; but they also sound utopian and hard to understand for average people, whether conservative, liberal, or apolit-ical. Other comments are quite modest, such as "support-ing human rights," which was briefly a goal of the Carter administration. Similarly, "assisting Russia and Israel in moving to better governments" is so vague as to be unclear since both governments in power were strongly buttressed by the United States at the time. On corporate control, Nader was much clearer:

> "Global corporations are sucking the life out of small businesses and family farms. Pollution is poisoning our rivers and air. Inner-city schools and health clinics are crumbling. And while the nation cor-rodes, the rich are buying and selling pol-iticians like baseball cards. Big business is on a collision course with American democracy, and American democracy has been losing," said Mr. Nader. (Dao 2000)

Yet what to do about such a huge and overwhelming situation is not clear. Not mentioning overthrowing capitalism, his On the Issues site mentions many things, but what to do?

- 1960s seatbelt laws represented a cultural change. (Nov 2008)
- Washington DC is corporate-occupied territory. (Feb 2008)
- Obama & McCain differ, but neither takes on corporations. (Feb 2008)
- Democracy is gone when elections are commercialized. (Jan 2008)
- Corporations have too much control over people's lives. (Jan 2008)
- Corporations control government; that defines fascism. (Jan 2008)
- Citizenship agenda for cracking down on corporate crime. (Oct 2004)
- No eminent domain gifts to private enterprises. (Aug 2004)
- Legislative action should make rights for consumers, not corporations. (Jul 2004)
- Economic powers control our lives and our elections. (Jul 2004)

- Capitalism can lead to fascism. (Jul 2004)
- Corporations should not legally be counted as individuals. (Jul 2004)
- Giant corporations roam the Earth making people into serfs. (Jul 2004)
- Corporate politics is only free speech because money talks. (Oct 2002)
- Major parties both focus on wealthy interests. (Oct 2002)
- Net worth is $3.8 million; owns corporate stocks. (Oct 2002)
- Consumerism is about corporations vs. citizens. (Sep 2002)
- Shift power from corporations to consumers. (Oct 2000)
- 1995: Gov. Bush's tort reform benefited him personally. (Aug 1999)
- Ethical rules should REQUIRE reporting corporate misconduct. (Dec 1998)
- Legal delaying tactics cause crisis in confidence in law. (Dec 1998)
- Corporate state gives away public assets to private monopoly. (Dec 1998)

This list, evidently a highlight of Nader's many statements from 1998 to 2008 on corporations, is mostly statements of fact (in his opinion, of course). There are almost no prescriptive demands here. One can glean demands for stricter ethics rules, opposition to court decisions to consider corporations as people for speech rights, more consumer rights, and campaign financial reform. But these are in response to statements like "Washington DC is corporate-occupied territory," "Corporations have too much control over people's lives," "Economic powers control our lives and our elections," "Capitalism can lead to fascism," and "Giant corporations roam the earth, making people into serfs." And finally, how do we shift power from corporations to consumers? No hint is given.

There is a huge disjuncture between diagnosis and lack of remedy here, while with the foreign policy example, there was almost the opposite—a naive faith that under some sort of new leadership, the United States could start anew as a humanitarian world leader. But really, as we have seen, they are not that contradictory. Progressives are middle-class reformers draped in the language of radicalism at times but are nowhere close to being real radicals, much less revolutionaries. Their optimism entails the desire to change both states and systems and millions of people at a fell swoop, which cannot really occur. The fact is, as in the Jackson campaign, Nader's broad statements are followed by smaller piecemeal reforms, although many theorists have thought about these issues. Many nations, both socialist and social democratic, have sought to implement varieties of corporate control involving worker control and public control, but we see no reflection about them[10]. But in addition to the huge discrepancies on issues, Nader really never proceeded to be a party alternative to the two main parties. In fact, he suggested several times that voters might vote for Democratic candidates not for president:

> "Politically, Mr. Nader's message is a bit complicated. He says that he hopes his candidacy will energize turnout for Democratic candidates in close races for the House of Representatives, and thus help turn power over to House Democratic leaders, and away from the Republicans in the House leadership whom he calls beyond the pale." (Verhovek 2000)

> "He even made what sounded like a pitch for Democratic Congressional candidates, urging voters in districts where no Green Party candidates are running to support

'the most progressive candidates.'" (Dao 2000)

Nader clearly made visible his status as a disgruntled liberal whose objective was not a new party or a new radicalization but merely his own quest for the presidency and hostility to Democratic candidate Albert Gore. While few in Congress supported much of Nader's thinking, presumably, he favored voters supporting their local and state Democratic parties. But second, Nader never embraced any strategy that would develop a new radical party. His relationship with the Green Party was tenuous at best, and he rarely spoke about it. According to insiders, Nader neither joined the Green Party nor shared his donor/volunteer list with them (Hardy 2008). Neither he nor the party developed methods to increase, at a local level, the activists who could constitute a future party that might be stronger. Indeed, Nader ran in 2004 and 2008 only as an independent without Green backing. While he received 2.7 percent of the vote in 2000 (actually more than Henry Wallace in 1948), he declined to only 0.038 percent in 2004 and 0.056 percent in 2008. While many reasons are cited for Nader's decline, chiefly the anger and frustration at the close election of 2000 and Nader's possible spoiler role as a third-party candidate, it is hard to see why more people would flock to his candidacy in any event. As with most progressives, little separated him from liberalism; and as the Democratic Party at least got slightly more liberal by the time of Obama, there was little political space left. Nor had any grassroots local organization been created that could debate positions or learn from mistakes and/or propose new approaches since the Greens were minimal in numbers and Nader then had no party.

More Powerful than Elections?

It might be noted that while Ralph Nader's candidacy became an afterthought quickly after 2000, the Battle of Seattle, as it was called, in which forty thousand demonstrators stopped the World Trade Organization meeting and paralyzed Seattle, Washington, for several days in late November and early December 1999, made far more of impact. At least, for a few years, the prospect worldwide of a coalition of labor, environmentalists, radicals of all sorts, students, religious leaders, farmers, and others disrupting the worldwide financial dealings of the elites struck fear among the leaders. But even the left's accounts of the Seattle protest focused on the wrong things: it was not "Teamsters and Turtles," as the popular phrase was coined (see Berg 2003), but the organization and strategy of seasoned radicals and groups of anarchists that succeeded. While, of course, it is important to have a coalition, neither the environmentalists dressed as sea turtles nor husky Teamster members who were told which march to go to and which to avoid accounted for the power of what the group did, which was shut down part of Seattle, Washington. This is power, and it is a power that the left, far more than liberals or others, potentially has. That it does not do so is subject to political socialization toward being correct model citizens, the emphasis on electoral politics, and of course, plain fear of police and government surveillance organizations. Nevertheless, it is important to note this power, which was missing after the early days of Occupy Wall Street! in 2011. They failed to think strategically about how to use the people power, and they had lacked a way to have an impact on the system. As we move to the current time, there is little difference between the Sanders-and-Warren progressive approach and the Jackson-and-Nader approach. All have consumed progressives with electoral strategies to the detriment of other strategies.

FIVE

Progressives IV: More Progressive than Thou

Anti-Trumpism is not a politics.

—Mark Lilla,
The Once and Future Liberal

Such is the US left's worldview. It is also a measure of its intellectual poverty. Whatever liberals are smoking, it is no stimulant to new ideas.

—Edward Luce,
The Retreat of Western Liberalism

Despite how contemporaries may feel, the last decade and a half has really added little new to America's mainstream political gridlock or to the strategies of progressives. Rather, as progressives replace liberals within the Democratic Party, they have found a home, albeit with occasional grumbling, in the mainstream world of politics. Of course, this is not so different from the days of Theodore Roosevelt or the Popular Front of the 1930s and 1940s. Never politically radical, it is not very surprising that progressives felt at home with Barack Obama, although he did not call himself a progressive or accomplish much to earn the label of a progressive president. Rather, each election season (which seems almost always now), battles over "who is more progressive than whom?" occur, with Obama versus Hillary Clinton in 2008, Clinton versus Bernie Sanders in 2016, the current Democratic race with Sanders, and Elizabeth Warren against moderates such as Joe Biden. As an active left involved in street protest or organizing communities or workplaces receded other than the occasional march to oppose the archvillain President Donald Trump, vanishes, no matter who wins the next election, the long-term tradition of an oppositional left vanishes into history.

This chapter will review briefly the candidacy and presidency of Obama, the Clinton-Sanders 2016 campaign, the election of Donald Trump, and the quick decline of street protests to resume campaigning for Congress and the presidency respectively in 2018 and for 2020. In chapter 6,

I will return to broader points about not only progressives but also the failure of any left to emerge for many years and how, unfortunately, in my view, this fact is not an American exceptionalism but a worldwide phenomenon after the collapse of both communism and social democracy. There are some issues I identify that limit the possibilities of a vibrant left at this time.

Clinton versus Obama: Will the Real Progressive Please Stand Up?

The irony of the primaries of 2008, which spent so many millions of dollars and so much time, is that ultimately, it is not clear that either candidate Barack Obama or Hillary Clinton was very progressive. Yet in somewhat of a change from the campaigns of the 1990s and early 2000s, the Democratic Party voters had become more liberal and tired of the (Bill) Clintonesque centrism carried out by Bill, Al Gore, and others. No doubt the great divide over the Iraqi War was a factor.

Obama was like the Teflon man in the campaign and his presidency. Attractive, articulate, and African-American, Obama was greeted as a new prince of politics—a combination of Eisenhower's above-the-fray image and the vitality of JFK. Indeed, Obama insisted, despite his liberal record, that

> "he can transcend the starkly red-and-blue politics of the last 15 years, end the partisan and ideological wars and build a new governing majority. To achieve the change the country wants, he says, 'we need a leader who can finally move beyond the divisive politics of Washington and bring Democrats, independents and Republicans together to get things done.'" (Toner 2008)

Promising, in the words of George W., to be a "uniter, not a divider," Obama's

> "rise has been built in part on the idea that he represents a break from the established identities that have defined many of the nation's divisions. To many, he embodies a promise to bridge black and white, old and young, rich and poor— and Democrats, Republicans and independents." (ibid.)

Yet ironically, Obama had among the most liberal records in the Senate, and the record of Hillary Clinton was not strikingly different. The *National Journal* found "that of 267 measures on which both voted that Obama and Clinton differed on only 10" (ibid.). In fact, the *New York Times* columnist and economist Paul Krugman found Clinton the more liberal, though he did not necessarily support this with facts. He called her proposals "surprisingly bold and progressive," while Obama's "actual policy proposals, though liberal, tended to be cautious and relatively orthodox" (Krugman 2008). Writing in June 2008, Krugman realized that progressive activists were voting for Obama rather than Clinton, but he kept up his opinion (this was indeed correct) that Obama was a centrist and Clintonesque. He correctly called that his views, "particularly on health care, were often to the right of his rivals" (Krugman 2008). He also anticipated the future by noting he "had outraged progressives by supporting a wiretapping bill, that, among other things, grants immunity to telecom companies for any illegal acts they may have undertaken at the Bush administration's behest." We now know that Obama was being logical. After all, he continued, as revealed by Edward Snowden in 2013, Bush's surveillance program on American citizens that the Democrats had criticized.

Obama's victory in the primaries, no doubt, came from his charismatic style. The fact that he was the first African-American to be a serious candidate for president and his anti-war stand in Iraq seemed to qualify him as a progressive and make him an easy choice over Hillary Clinton. Whether Obama would have won the 2008 election without the economic collapse of that year may be debated. The vote was not overwhelming, and the McCain-Palin ticket did not take the hearts of America, so it can be argued either way.

The Cooling-Off of the Obama Love Affair

By several years later (as is so common in America), many people had cooled on Obama and criticized his conservatism. The Occupy Wall Street movement beginning in October 2011 sharply criticized the president. Kevin Zeese, who organized a protest in October 2011 that drew five hundred people to New York City's Chamber of Commerce with signs like "No More Wall Street White House," said, "There's a lot of discontent with Obama's policies. Obama is out of touch. He's busy going around the country raising $1 billion to run for re-election" (Landler 2011). This was among the milder statements. Bill Brunot, a mechanical engineer from Winchester, Virginia, and Occupy! protestor noted, "With the people he put in, Goldman Sachs basically occupies the White House. We got sold out; the banks got bailed out!" (ibid.). Erika Hoffman of Occupy! accused him of constantly siding with Wall Street. She was angry. "This person [Obama] touched the hearts of people who needed change and hope. I think he let everybody down" (Mala 2012). Even the *New York Times* columnists voiced displeasure with Obama's policies. In a June 2012 article, Ross Douthat wrote that

> "apart from his disavowal of waterboarding (an interrogation practice the Bush White House had already abandoned), almost the entire Bush-era wartime architecture has endured: rendition is still with us, the Guantanamo detention center is still open, drone strikes have escalated dramatically, and the Obama White House has claimed the right—and, in the case of Anwar al-Awlaki, followed through on it—to assassinate American citizens without trial. These moves have met some principled opposition from the left. But the president's liberal critics are usually academics, journalists and (occasionally)

cable-TV hosts, with no real mass constituency behind them." (Douthat 2012)

Perhaps what was most striking—and this says a lot about America's two-party system and its followers—was the fact that Democrats, for the most part, had followed Obama's foreign policy lead:

> "The majority of Democrats, polls suggest, have followed roughly the same path as the former Yale Law School dean Harold Koh, a staunch critic of Bush's wartime policies who now serves as a legal adviser to the State Department, supplying constitutional justifications for Obama's drone campaigns. What was outrageous under a Republican has become executive branch business-as-usual under a Democrat." (ibid.)

Then we must mention the so-called signature policy of the Obama presidency, the Affordable Care Act. I must say that as a professor of social policy for thirty years, I have not witnessed as much hostility toward or praise for so little reform. First, Obama stole the plan—pretty much lock, stock, and barrel—from Republican Mitt Romney who passed an almost identical measure in Massachusetts (ironically because the GOP had staked out a position totally against the ACA by 2012, he could not really take credit for it). Second, one would wonder what kind of plan would enlist the support of the pharmaceutical and insurance industry, the Chamber of Commerce, the hospital industry, and other health providers. Of course, only a plan that would give them millions more customers to boost their profits with limited costs. Matt Taibbi's *Griftopia* (2011) provides the most lively, incisive account of the negotiations and corporate high jinx that gave us the ACA; but Bill Scher, in his July 2012 the *New York Times* piece, followed why "many progressives, frustrated over the past three years have concluded the political system is fundamentally broken because corporate power has been allowed to suffocate popular liberal policies" (Scher 2012). Of course, one of his examples of business as usual was the ACA, which newly revealed (at the time) emails between the White House and the pharmaceutical lobby showed many of the trade-offs. Obama promised lobbyists a "direct line of communication," and he suggested they "stay quiet" about an agreement to "bury a proposal for cheap drug imports." He was persuaded to abandon any public option for health care by the promise that the drug companies would pay for pro-reform advertisements (ibid.). So desperate was Obama and his advisers for a victory on health care (not wishing to suffer the ignominy of Bill Clinton's defeat in 1993) that basically he gave away much of the store in return for the concessions to allow coverage for those with preexisting conditions and to allow children to be placed on their parents' plans until twenty-six. This was much of the sum and substance of health-care reform, which did not settle any of the major problems of the American health system but basically kicked the can down the road. Of course, the American people ended up split on the policy since it did not offer much to some people, but naturally others felt a little change was better than none. Only the Democratic Party politicians attempted to portray it (pretty unsuccessfully) as a major triumph.

So, with all the hoopla about the Obama administration in eight years of office (as Krugman predicted), the nation got another centrist like Bill Clinton. The Obama administration was involved in seven wars (he was the "peace candidate"), followed mostly the Bush foreign policy, and other than a few executive orders, did not do much on domestic issues.

Sanders against Clinton: A Tale of Two Progressives

The 2016 campaign brought an even more bitter battle of the progressives with the candidacy of Vermont senator Bernie Sanders, threatening the presumed nominee, now Hillary Clinton. By the New Hampshire primary, the two tossed the term *progressive* at each other. Sanders proclaimed the following:

> "Mrs. Clinton's credentials as a progressive [are questionable] … her views on foreign policy, trade, the environment and money in politics separated her from those lawmakers who proudly wear that label … (Sanders) suggested that Mrs. Clinton's positions sometimes shifted depending on her venue. 'You can't say you're a moderate on one day and be a progressive on another day,' he said, noting that Mrs. Clinton described herself as a moderate last year. 'You can't be a moderate and a progressive. They're different.'" (Rappeport 2016)

Clinton's response relied not on specific social policies but on personalities. She claimed, by Sanders's definition, that

> "Obama or vice-president Joseph R. Biden would not be considered progressive. I am a progressive who likes to get things done. I was somewhat amused that Senator Sanders has set himself up as the gatekeeper of who gets to be a progressive." (ibid.)

Typically, the progressive-label battle was mostly an argument over symbolism. Sanders accused Clinton of being a patron of Wall Street with her own super PAC (Political Action Committee) and hundreds of thousands of dollars paid to her for speeches at companies like Goldman Sachs. In return, Clinton had even less substance in her returns. Clinton countered that Sanders's characterization was "a low blow" and that she had stood for "gay and women's rights around the world" (ibid.). The latter claim is hard to verify because Hillary had not even supported gay marriage until 2013, and she can be seen as, at best, a rather moderate to liberal feminist.

Stepping back, of course, there is no question that Sanders came from the left, while Clinton had traveled from deep in the establishment. Identifying himself as a leftist for forty years, Sanders had found his way to the Democratic Party after many years as an independent from Vermont as a mayor, congressman, and then senator. He proclaimed himself a democratic socialist, a term he has never clearly defined. But compared to Sanders, Clinton had little claim on the progressive vote except that she was a woman, the first with a major chance for the presidency. She often tried to move the subject to identity politics. To the leftish voters who had felt locked out by the Obama administration and then the failure of Occupy Wall Street to generate any lasting movement, Sanders was a hero. The *New York Times* quoted a supporter saying, "The Sanders movement brought Occupy Wall Street into Democratic Party presidential politics. He occupied the Democratic primaries" (Mahler and Alcindor 2016).

Yet despite his far better performance than expected in the primaries, there is little reason to see the vote as any endorsement of democratic socialism. Clinton again (as in 2008) was a decidedly non-charismatic campaigner with little appeal to the younger generation and a symbol to many of them of the rich and powerful. Nevertheless, Michael Lind, writing in the *New York Times,* noted probably correctly that Clintonism remained the direction of the party. First, noting the power of identity politics, which will be addressed further in chapter 6, Lind argues that a safe neoliberalism probably was more favorable to most Democrats than any redistribution of income as hinted at (but never fully fleshed out) by Sanders:

> "The centrality of identity politics, rather than progressive economics, to the contemporary Democratic Party is nothing new. In 1982, the Democratic National Committee recognized seven official caucuses: women, blacks, Hispanics, Asians, gays, liberals and business/professionals. Thirty-four years later, this is the base of the Democratic Party of Hillary Clinton. The pro-Sanders left objects to the solicitude of the Democratic Party for Wall Street and Silicon Valley, the sources of much of its funding. But it is safe to assume that most progressives, when confronted with conservative candidates, will prefer incremental, finance-friendly Clintonism over the right-wing alternative. Moreover, the ability or even willing-

ness of Mr. Sanders to help down-ballot or state candidates is doubtful. The next generation of Democrats are figures like Julian and Joaquin Castro and Senator Cory Booker of New Jersey, who are much more in the mold of the Clintons and Mr. Obama than of the maverick outsider Bernie Sanders." (Lind 2016)

His prediction of the reign of Clintonism, if not Clinton, seems to me, as I shall discuss later, to be applicable already to this election period (2020), which at least two progressive candidates still find many Democrats opposed to them, and the proposals themselves (like Medicare for All) are less than wildly popular:

"Most important of all, it would be a serious mistake to assume that the growing sympathy of many of today's millennials for the concept of democratic socialism as embodied by Mr. Sanders will translate into a social democratic America in the 2030s or 2050s. Half a century ago, as the Age of Aquarius gave way to the Age of Reagan, many of the hippies of the '60s became, in effect, the yuppies of the '80s—still socially liberal, but with new concerns about government spending, now that they were paying taxes and mortgages." (ibid.)

Two other articles that appeared in the *New York Times* that spring hit on problems faced by progressives going back to 1912 and 1924 and continuing today. One is the failure of the Sanders movement to build a national organization not just to elect him but also to fight for an actual base of possible supporters who would run for office at a local and state level and, perhaps, heaven forbid, do some other things like actual organizing. Mahler and Alcindor (2016) quoted Howard Dean, former governor of Vermont, on the difference between one election and having an "on-the-ground machine that delivers." He noted there: "There have to be candidates who are supported. There have to be issues that are put forward. There have to be opportunities to put pressure on legislators. That is not the same thing as a political campaign."

Mahler and Alcindor noted the following:

"Thus far, Mr. Sanders has offered little support for a broader progressive movement, beyond using his email list to solicit money for a handful of congressional candidates, including Washington State's Pramila Jayapal, New York's Zephyr Teachout and Nevada's Lucy Flores. Even if he does try to redirect the energy behind his candidacy into a new liberal organization, the task may not be easy. His campaign has brought together disparate individuals and volunteer groups that might be inclined to go their separate ways after the primary. His regular diatribes against the influence of big money in politics could make it awkward, if not impossible, for him to raise money from wealthy liberals." (ibid.)

An article by Mark Schmitt (2016), though he does not go into great detail, hints at the other continuing problem for progressives. Though their program remains vague, their possible promise of redistributing income throughout society is not necessarily popular. Schmitt argues that Sanders's political views were more from the past than current. Schmitt gives an example of health insurance:

"For example, many liberal Democrats would agree with Mr. Sanders, in theory, that single-payer health insurance could be fairer, more efficient and cheaper than our fragmented system. But the president and Congress made the decision in 2010 to build on the private insurance system, in the form of the Affordable Care Act, in part because single-payer wasn't politically viable. A Democratic administration's next moves will be to expand and strengthen the Affordable Care Act, not start over." (Schmitt 2016)

Reviewing other issues like the reform of Wall Street and the minimum wage, Schmitt argues that rather than redistribution of income, most progressives (here he views progressive think tanks and congresspeople as leaders) reject the approach:

"This difference is part of a larger gap between Mr. Sanders and other progressives in their approaches to economic inequality. Where Mr. Sanders talks about 'redistribution' of wealth from 'the billionaires' to the middle- and low-income classes through high tax rates, others, such as the economists at the Economic Policy Institute, have focused more on what is sometimes called redistribution- wages and the conditions of work. They would reduce the gains at the top—such as by putting some meaningful constraints on executive pay—but also make sure that workers got a greater share of the profits, not only in the form of money, but also time, flexibility and predictable scheduling. If the initial distribution of benefits and money is badly skewed, it will be hard to use tax and transfer policies alone to redistribute it."

Although Schmitt is correct, we end up with a kind of syllogism: Sanders was to the left of the Democratic Party; hence, he is to the left of it. Perhaps an honest approach would have been to run as an independent. Sanders could not really criticize Clintonism or Obamaism and be a Democratic nominee. So, he answered a question about (Bill) Clinton's presidency by saying "he did some good things" lukewarmly. The real problem for progressives is

Americans' uncertainty on what redistribution means and how it would be done and how a view favoring such efforts would affect America. Since the progressives' strategies boil down to running for office and being pretty quiet about socialist tendencies (Sanders included), they lose any opportunity to educate people, which is one of the claims some people make for running. Rather than an ongoing campaign and organizing strategy that might change the political culture, the local organizing culture, and the way opinion is shaped, they find in the one-shot election campaigns that they represent a minority. Again and again, as La Follette, Wallace, Jackson, Nader, and Sanders illustrate, there are strong limits to educating Americans through a political campaign. In my view, only sharing the experience of workers at their workplaces, tenants in their neighborhoods, congregants at religious services, for example, rather than egoistically beg for their votes will influence long-term opinion.

The Trump Era: The Daily Battle

Although contemporaries sometimes overstate current events, I do think it is a good characterization of the period from Trump's election to now (as I write) as being quite unique. America has had less than great presidents many times but never has someone been so visibly personally incompetent and perhaps seriously psychiatrically troubled. He has blundered and blustered his way through each day with tweets that condemn various people, sometimes his allies as well as enemies. His speeches and some of his views make many Americans shudder, and of course, he is fairly open with his sexism, racism, and anti-immigrant views if not a few other prejudices.

Having said this, Trump is not a fascist—as progressives labeled him—or even on the extreme right. Ronald Reagan was much more of an ideologue than Trump and, by the way, far more of a threat to the left than Trump. In fact, Trump is liberal on social welfare and has fought NAFTA, which was a left-wing target, and has agreed (although not done anything yet) that the US wars should end. He carries the right-wing water on cultural issues such as abortion and gun rights and has made relatively conservative Supreme Court choices. But like a lot of Republicans confirmed to the Supreme Court, the two newest judges, Gorsuch and Kavanaugh, will have their own views with lifetime tenure. There is already no evidence that Gorsuch is a hard-right justice, and Kavanaugh may not be. The only other act that Trump has had passed was his tax cut, which was criticized as a break for the rich and did not differ very much from Kennedy and Reagan's tax-cut measures. There have been areas of tough talk, like on immigration, but judges and Congress have blocked most implementation. But further, it is only the most naive who believe in the capitalist, imperialist system of the world and that an individual is the key problem. The left struggles to explain when life was good, certainly not under the array of presidents before Trump.

Unfortunately, the decision of the progressives and the Democratic Party to resist Trump has created its own problems. We have heard on a daily basis a barrage of attacks—some well-taken positions, but some off-the-wall. One cannot turn on the news networks or read most newspapers without it being "Trump and anti-Trump all night long" or "every page." Most of the country is in some ways more mature than the media and politicians and ignores this daily fray. The Democratic Party and progressives only live for the next election, and unfortunately, this makes for actions that will hurt them in the long term. As the impeachment effort goes on, two things are occurring: the most obvious is that people are getting annoyed and angry and, second, that those candidates busy on the 2020 campaign trail have lost much of their audience for proposals. Many people do not know there is a debate about health care, for example, as the daily news features Trump or Democratic leaders Nancy Pelosi, Charles Schumer, and Adam Schiff again and again. Of course, mainstream Democrats may like this since many centrists, like Joe Biden, do not have much of a program (like Obama); and so he may hope to have a victory based on the developments by 2020 that have nothing to do with policy. The continual anti-Trump chorus actually hurts those like Warren and Sanders most as they want to discuss social policy.

Very early after the election, many warned about such a course. Leonard Pitts's March 2017 column quoted two of them:

> "Joan Blades, co-founder of the liberal activist group MoveOn.org, wrote an essay for *The Christian Science Monitor*, asking progressives to stretch beyond their left-wing comfort zones and 'love thy neighbor.' And *New York Times* columnist Nicholas Kristof warned the left against a tendency to 'otherize' Donald Trump voters." (Pitts 2017)

As quoted in the front of the chapter, Mark Lilla (2017) warned that anti-Trumpism was not a politics, and Edward Luce (2018) warned that "to write off all those who voted for him [Trump] as bigoted will only make his job easier. It is also inaccurate. Millions who backed Trump in 2016 voted for Obama in 2008 … by giving a higher priority to the politics of ethnic identity than people's common interests, the American Left helped to create what it feared." (Luce, p. 95)

It was very clear that the 2016 election was about social class, with Trump winning the white working class and Clinton the middle classes and also African-American and (to a lesser margin) Hispanic/Latino vote. It would have made sense to take the opportunity of there being no election in 2017 to attempt to heal wounds and to, as we would say in the 1960s and 1970s, organize the white working class. While some did, this was not the main thrust of the Democratic Party allied progressives.

The Battle of Progressives Rejoined: The Election Season

Though in 2017, activists and the news media gloated over how much the Trump election was uniting the opposition, in fact, the only unity would be anti-Trump; and by 2018, they were fully guided by the Democratic Party to be an electoral movement. In a laudatory *Los Angeles Times* article in April 2017, Mascaro (2017) claimed that

> "President Trump's election has mobilized thousands of first-time activists in a do-it-yourself movement like nothing seen on the political left in years. With bountiful energy and some impressive early successes, the grass-roots movement has stunned even Democratic Party officials, drawing comparisons to the tea party movement that transformed the GOP with its unyielding opposition after President Obama's election."

These great claims over a less than four-month period seem rather grand. Perhaps, the only point that is worth noting is the fear on the part of the Democratic Party that they could not control the movement:

> "But privately, many Democrats also worry the movement is whipping up a deep-rooted emotional and ideologi-

cal fervor, much like the tea party did in blocking Obama's agenda. Unpredictable and with no clear leadership, the liberal uprising could prove difficult to contain and may turn its anger—currently focused on Trump—toward the Democratic Party itself, just as the tea party fractured the GOP." (ibid.)

In actuality, the early demonstrations and harsh language against not only Trump but also some Democratic Party leaders would fade early on.

Another early article, breathless in its excitement for the new activism against Trump, was Tim Dickinson's in the *Rolling Stone* (2017). Praising the new groups such as Indivisible, Swing Left, and Our Revolution seemed to play to its leftish audience by noting how some of the groups saw themselves as Democrats and some not. Again, taking the Tea Party as a close movement, the article held out hope for great things but ignored the lack of real independence of these groups politically.

By midterm election time in 2018, almost all vestiges of any independent movement had faded. Even in California, one of the deepest of blue states and a center of the early airport demonstrations against banning immigrants and other anti-Trump rallies, very little remained outside the Democratic Party. Perhaps one can include the antifa movement, if it qualifies as big enough, that still came to disrupt right-wing rallies; and there were a few militant Black Lives Matter demonstrations. But for the most part, as usual, much activism stalled for election time.

Gaining a very large turnout for a midterm election, the Democrat Party did take up forty-one seats in the House, making it a majority, which was a large gain particularly in light of all the impeachment efforts that would occur. The Senate remained Republican with the GOP, in fact picking up two seats.

What became evident with the beginning of the large primary pool of Democratic candidates emerging was that the activism/militance seen by journalists such as Mascaro and Dickinson headed straight to the next election, mostly supporting Bernie Sanders or, a new favorite progressive, Sen. Elizabeth Warren of Massachusetts. While early on, Sen. Kamala Harris of California seemed a possibility, but she quit the race after her early good standing fell. As I write, polls show a very close race between moderate Joe Biden and Sanders and Warren and even ex-mayor of South Bend, Indiana, Peter Buttigieg. Some polls show Warren ahead at times.

Typical of progressive movements, which emphasize elections and policy papers over movements, there is little in the way of the policies advocated by Sanders and Warren that seem to be very realistic. In a clever article by David Brooks of the *New York Times* entitled "A Brief History of the Warren Presidency" (2019), Brooks predicts she will defeat Sanders for the nomination and go on to be president, even winning a majority in the Senate. While dance-in-the-streets euphoria greeted her election, the problems began when she sought to achieve any legislation:

> "One by one, her proposals failed in the Senate: Medicare for All, free college, decriminalizing undocumented border crossing, even the wealth tax. Democratic senators from red states, she learned, were still from red states; embracing her agenda would have been suicidal." (ibid.)

Brooks goes on to see a split between liberal and progressive Democrats, leading to war within the Democratic Party, and by 2030, progressive populism had died out as had right-wing populism.

While I do not share Brooks' prognostics, the key point I agree with is if by some chance Warren (or now

more likely Sanders) was elected, what would be the policy and political outcome? Medicare for All has dropped
to its lowest level of support in October 2019, with only
a narrow percentage supporting it (Zeballos-Roig 2019).
While the reasons are not totally clear, it appears that as
critics such as Biden and others have chipped at the proposal, they have fed the popular anxiety about change and
the fear they would not be able to keep their private insurance. As I have noted before, given how broad a change
Medicare For All would be and how opposed it is by most
of the medical community, it would take a landslide election not only for a president but also a Congress extremely
difficult to imagine composed of radicals, dare we say it, to
be considered. Much more likely, a Democratic presidency
and Congress would bring small changes in medical care
on the order of the ACA.

Some other proposals have more support. A recent
article (Doherty 2019) found that about 60 percent of
Americans felt the wealthy were not paying their fair share.
This would support a wealth tax, but again, given a likely
Congress, don't look for anything grand here, perhaps just
a change in the Trump tax reform. Perhaps the most support for a reform seems to be for free college tuition, but a
close look here as well (Campaign for Free College Tuition
2019) shows a much less generous plan to include only

state universities and to lodge it on the state, rather than federal level, is the most favored. As can be seen, it is hard to really describe this year as a big year of change. It is not the 1930s era of the Great Depression or the 1960s era of civil rights and support for some big government. There is little reason to believe that whoever wins office will have a mandate (or probably a drive) to make big changes.

Meanwhile, a little closer in time, we have seen what seems to be an inexorable move to impeachment. The nation has been split in polls, 50-50 percent, on the wisdom and validity of impeachment. But Democratic leadership seems to have chosen its road. It may or may not succeed, and it may not succeed politically if it does in Congress. There will be many people sympathetic to the president; others, just angry at the continued gridlock. No doubt, whatever the result, the media and parties will call for "healing" and an end to division perhaps afterward, turning to moderates like Biden. Also, in a closely divided electorate, there is always a possibility of independents and nonvoters changing the fractions each party holds. Based on social media, I can say that independents seem to be growing as well as the advocacy of boycotting elections.

Progressives = Liberals with Attitude!

I have concluded the chronological description of progressives from the 1900s to today. While there are, of course, always specific tendencies in each historical period, as I suggested, there is considerable continuity in the style and substance of progressives from the early Progressive movement to today's (rhetorically) militant, self-described progressives.

I dub this as being liberals with attitude because at least since the 1930s Popular Front, progressives have paired a liberal to left-liberal Democratic Party program with a tendency to loud rhetoric and self-righteousness that comes from knowing one is right. There is a sense in middle-class reform, always, that educated people who have studied the facts have a more refined and certain position than those who are not. This hubris marries some of the righteousness that the old left of Stalinism had, which is its penchant for dialectics and historical progress. There is a deep confusion, generally in America, between those who talk loudest or yell more fulsomely at rallies are somehow radical as compared with those who do not. Hence, the attitude of progressives toward those who do not share their views is not *liberal* in the first meaning of the word—"benevolent or open"—but one of hostility. This hostility greets not only conservatives but also those who do not completely agree with their views. If you have the temerity of saying you are not voting or voting for a third party, look out for militant liberals and progressives. I must say I have never had the experience of being intimidated by a conservative or moderate in this fashion.

On the other hand, progressives claim the mantle of a left. It is not entirely clear where this mantle comes from, whether the days of Popular Front or the lack of a real presence of a left in the USA in recent decades (see chapter 6). Yet progressives tend to be convinced that elections and the ability to write legislation or policy papers are the sine qua non of politics, but again, this represents a middle-class educated school of people who have had too many political science or social policy classes. Movements, grassroots organizing, and the politics of nations cannot be reduced to rationalism that can be demonstrated by a social planner or a policy analyst. Much of politics is not rational, but a matter of feelings aroused in different regions and people of the country, many of whom do not even care to vote. It is hard for progressives to see a way to influence the broader mass other than to say "vote" to everyone, despite the general failure of this action to produce much for Americans, particularly in the lower classes. As long as large numbers of working and poorer people are detached from politics, and perhaps also resentful of their higher class's dominance in politics, the more difficult it will be to change anything. Yet progressives seem undisturbed by a purely electoral politics in which they pray for their candidates each election year as if Nirvana was around the corner. Having been blinded by their ideology as are others, progressives do the same thing over the years. Presenting their ideas and candidates as new, they involve similar reforms and policies as the last time around.

Democrats as the Party of Finance and Technology

Interestingly, as more progressives align with the Democratic Party, the old critique of big money has faded away from their critique. With each year, the Democratic Party raises more money; and in 2018, for the first time in recent history, they raised more money than the Republicans. A report from the Public Citizen (Shaw 2019) showed enormous funds being raised for the political campaigns in 2017–18. Seeming to ignore how excited some of their peers are with big money, Robert Weissman, the president of Public Citizen criticized "lavish spending on both Republicans and Democrats, the ultrawealthy receive access and influence to block the aggressive, progressive policy agenda that Americans favor by overwhelming margins. Our democracy cannot function if the plutocrat class maintains an iron grip on American election campaigns."

Yet what is interesting is, this massive amount of money is being thrown around by Democrat Party activists, most of them hedge fund managers. Public Citizen shows the financial industry represented 74% of funding for pro-Democratic outside spending efforts, followed by inherited wealth (8%), technology (6%), media (5%), and real estate (3%). By contrast, funding for pro-Republicans reflected "more industries, including gambling (41%), finance (25%), industrial supply and distribution (13%), energy (6%), and technology (2.6%)."

As Shaw himself notes, "the Democratic Party has generally been deferential to the finance industry and its policy wishes in recent history, and its dependence on the industry for election funding creates conflict of interest that makes significant change difficult." Thus far, the 2020 campaign seems to be replicating the earlier years.

An early list of Democratic donors shows $10 million for Tom Steyer's various hedge funds, $7.1 million for Donald Sussman of Paloma Partners (he is also the husband of Maine congresswoman Chellie Pingree), over $6 million from the perennial financier George Soros's funds, and $3.4 million from Renaissance Technologies, also a hedge fund—all to the Democrats. According to *Business Insider* (Court and Feinstein 2019), the health-care sector has already made contributions to nearly all the 2020 candidates: Donald Trump, $1.4 million; Pete Buttigieg, $544 million; Kamala Harris, $517 million; Joe Biden, $456 million; Bernie Sanders, $360 million; Elizabeth Warren, $344 million; Cory Booker, $305 million; Beto O'Rourke, $255 million; Amy Klobuchar, $209 million; and Julián Castro, $123 million. Another list of individuals to the 2018 campaign shows not only Steyer, Sussman, Soros, and Simons' Renaissance Technology but also Mike Bloomberg at $94 million (also from finance capital), Fred Eychaner of Newsweb in Chicago, Jeff Bezos of Amazon (though he also gave to Republicans), and Reid Hoffman of LinkedIn (Center for Responsive Politics and OpenSecrets.com).

We have the liberal/progressives claiming the mantle of social change along with increasingly large sums of money being raised from finance capital and high technology companies. It seems, if anyone is in any doubt about what is in store for America if the Democratic Party win (and if the Republicans win), little change can really be expected. Monies given will likely continue the freedom from regulation and taxation for the high technology and investment industries, and money given to all candidates for health care will be for some form of milder health-care reform than a universal single-payer health care.

Summary

Before moving on to the state of the left as a whole in chapter 6, it is important to see how consistent the twentieth and early twenty-first century history of progressivism is. It is characterized by the following:

1. A naive faith in the will of the people to easily overcome entrenched interests and the power of big business.
2. A strategy narrowly focused on conventional politics focused on elections. Extra-legal and extra-conventional strategies are avoided in accordance with not offending middle-class norms.
3. A commitment for 120 years to dominant political parties. In the early twentieth century, this was the Republican Party of Theodore Roosevelt; but

since the mid-1930s, it has been the Democratic Party of Roosevelt, Clinton, Obama, and Biden and Sanders.

4. A commitment to vagueness in ideas and policy plans. Progressives, in order to keep a new popular front, need to obscure the line between conventional liberalism and radicalism such as the ideologies of socialism, Marxism, anarchism, and so on. While greatly opportunist (hoping to get radicals to vote with them), they have come to believe their own nostrums and become basically liberals with attitude!

5. Key to their esprit de corps is a dogmatism as profound as the old Communist Party from which they do have a historical debt (not only from the Popular Front but also from the party's historic backing of the Democratic Party). Although other parts of the political spectrum can be dogmatic, at times, progressives advance a desire to shut off dissent in their ranks and among viewpoints.

SIX

The Left: Left Behind?

Many nonfiction books about politics or social policy end with some optimism or at least proposals or suggestions for social change that would help alleviate social problems. When writing about social issues or problems, critics and theorists often believe they see a solution, at least, they can put on paper, which will help resolve these issues. This is not that type of book. Progressivism, in my view, is at best a mild reformist version of the left that has come to the fore again as a result of the erosion of an older left. It has historically been ineffective, and in my view, it will fail in its current incarnation, whether it wins elections or not. Its raison d'être has become a place in the Democratic Party. Unfortunately, we are at a time when, around the world, the right wing is ascendant and the left shows little sign of being able to fight it. In countries most known for their left opposition, such as those of France and Italy, the left seems defeated; and this process seems to be happening across many nations of the world. But in order to understand why, we have to describe the many failed ideas of the left as it emerged in nineteenth-century Europe as well as the added baggage that recent new social movements have placed on the rather already-creaky baggage of the older left. I will return to suggesting how some of these problems, while perhaps evident in the nature of earlier leftist movements, have become even worse in the period of progressive domination of the publications and messages of the left.

The Failed Left

Of course, there are many people for whom a left of any sort—radical, socialist, or progressive—was never attractive. Some of the areas discussed below—including the left's overly optimistic view of human nature, its over-commitment and almost love affair with the idea of the state, and its self-righteousness nature (aka now political correctness)—may well be reasons for their disaffection. But primarily, I wish to discuss here the disaffection of those who were left or might have been leftists but instead have retreated to liberalism or various states of being apolitical.

When I grew up in the 1960s and into the 1970s, despite the underdeveloped state of the American Left,[11] it was possible to be optimistic about the world's future.

Despite knowledge of faults of the Stalinist states like the Soviet Union and China, there was hope that the developing world's uprisings of the 1960s might change this. Moreover, the Soviet Union and China were supporting leftist movements around the world—from Indochina to Indonesia, Cuba to Chile, and France to South Africa (whether from just their own strategic interest or not). The direction of the world coming out of the period of decolonization seemed to be leftward. But well before the collapse of the Soviet Union and the fall of many organized parties of the left, there were warning signs that neither the old parties (the Communists and Social Democrats) nor the new ones of the New Left were doing very well. For example, in 1968, after a dramatic student uprising led to a general strike of workers in France, the left was incapable of capitalizing on a nation in turmoil; and a referendum backing De Gaulle's party ended the revolt. In the 1970s, many people on the left were excited by the democratic election (though by a slim margin) of Salvador Allende, a socialist who headed a peaceful transfer to what ostensibly would be socialism in Chile. Despite calls from leftist groups to arm the people, Allende refused and was toppled without huge resistance in 1973 by the Chilean military backed by the CIA. Then, of course, the victories of the left in the mid-1970s in Indochina, particularly Cambodia, stunned many sympathizers around the world. Even the most heinous tales of Stalinism did not prepare one for the sheer brutality and genocide of Pol Pot.

It was not long before the tide became even more obviously against the left. Nationalism seemed to trump left ideology in most places. China invaded Vietnam to keep them away from their borders. Right-wing military leaders besides Chile arose throughout Latin America in nations such as Argentina, Brazil, and Peru. The Soviet Union's ill-fated invasion of Afghanistan in 1979 would be their Vietnam. And by 1979–1980, with victories of Thatcher in the UK and Reagan in the US, the direction to the right seemed sealed.

What I am suggesting is, even before the fall of the Soviet Union and the decline of most European and many other nations' social democratic parties, the generalized vague hope for a unified left had failed. It was not just external events of the military coups or imperialism of the US (and Soviet Union). It was that middle-ground social democratic or the old-crusted communist parties were dead; they had failed. Either one responded to, say, the French failure after the general strike and the Chilean coup by becoming a mild liberal who would not chance general strikes and land takeovers (similar to the many US progressives) or one moved further to the left toward radical action common to, say, the anti-globalization movement activists or the anarchists. There seems no other way to go after abandoning social democracy and/or communism without going one way or the other (or, of course, to conservatism, moderation, or becoming apolitical). The rise of Pol Pots and, for that matter, the move to capitalism in China show that the mythology of a broad leftist unity based on a self-declared process of naming oneself as socialist or communist is a joke. Some new definitions of what a resistant left would be—both to capitalism and imperialism and to totalitarianism—is necessary.

The collapse of communism turned the Socialist and Communist parties of the world (with a few exceptions) into empty shells, some actually calling it quits. Contrary to American leftist predictions, particularly by groups like Democratic Socialists of America (DSA), the fall of communism did not bring new complete freedom and space for the left in Eastern Europe but led to a rise of the right and a nasty type of nationalism almost everywhere. We now have fairly overt fascist regimes in countries like Hungary and Poland, while other ex-communist bloc nations of Eastern Europe totter toward fascism. In Russia, we have the totalitarian and brutal Vladimir Putin whose regime makes even the post-Khrushchev regimes of the Soviet Union look good. Brazil and Philippines have extreme right-wing leaders. The so-called Arab Spring, which so excited people, led to authoritarian regimes in Egypt and brutal dictators like al-Assad in Syria murdering his own people. The United Kingdom, currently under Boris Johnson, is on the right, as is Italy, Austria, Greece, Australia, and India. Where there is a left, such as in Mexico and Spain (at least their presidents), it is sometimes hard to see what is being done, if anything, by them. Only in Latin America does the left appear to have some strength as recent riots in Ecuador and Chile indicate, as well as the recent victory in Argentina of the Peronist left.

There is much room for blame since it turns out neither countries with history of a true leftist movements nor neo-liberal nations like the USA with progressive movements have escaped the rightest trends. There are many avenues that can be examined (and in many cases have been), but there are some important points to be made about the fail-ure of the left.

Five Criticisms of the Left

(1) *The end of optimism.* The left myth, since at least Jean-Jacques Rousseau, that the popular will is virtuous and progressive has long been disproved. Nothing is really as central to leftist thinking than the ardent belief in the peo-

ple or masses or popular democracy or similar expressions. From at least the time of Jean-Jacques Rousseau, the left has taken hope in the popular will. Of course, barriers are acknowledged, such as ruling class ideology (which, alas, can take root in the commoners as well), petty bourgeois forces and ideology, peasant ideology, and effects of militarism, racism, and so on. Well, optimism, to some extent, could be justified in the days of the French Revolution and perhaps in Marx and Engels's days with the impact of the revolutions of 1848. But as historians know, whatever gains the left had achieved in the nineteenth and early twentieth century collapsed with World War I, overcame by nationalism, militarism, and hatred for others among the masses of Europe (led by most socialist Social Democratic parties). As we have seen, buttressed by the Great Depression of the 1930s, the left rose again; yet they somehow did not conclude after World War II that Nazism, Italian and Spanish fascism, Stalinism in the Soviet Union, Japanese militarism, and the use of the nuclear bomb were reasons to abandon optimism although, of course, many humble people and many intellectuals did. At least some who were progressive or radical left seemed to look ahead for renewed positive change. The belief in Hegelianism and Marxist dialectic and the progressive course of history has been an article of faith among leftists, whether they always state it or not. This is a Western prejudice with little support in history.

Well, if the 1930s and 1940s were not enough, what has been the trend today? Support of nationalism is world-wide (though the left does not support nationalism in theory when it sees the people as oppressed—it certainly does—violating its own precepts[12]); and violence, whether from random gun violence in the US to terrorism and war in other parts of the world, proceeds. People love to wave their nation's flags as they have over and over before; to hate those who are enemies, whether discriminated minorities or immigrants or people of different religions and with different political beliefs; and to have self-pride in themselves and their like-minded comrades. Over and over again, people of almost all nations have supported property rights, authoritarian power, and the ideas of both capitalism and totalitarianism. So much for the people's will!

Unfortunately, the left hides behind clichés and slogans to avoid confronting the sad human condition. I am amused at the chants like "This is what democracy looks like!" which began on the streets of Seattle, Washington, in 1999 or radio shows/websites like Amy Goodman's *Democracy Now!* Does the left really believe in democracy in which the right wing triumphs in many countries or virulent regimes around the world that initially, at least, are supported by their people? Why is it democratic when Obama wins the US presidency, but not when Trump (albeit in an electoral college vote) wins? When the United Kingdom votes for Brexit or Brazil for a right-wing dictator, the left seems to not believe it is democratic.

The left always comes up with contingent reasons: people were mad about this and that, they were unfairly influenced by mass media or the influence of the rich, or they acted out of racism and hatred. It does not take long to think of many reasons. But when something happens *over and over* and the thrust of world power and political discourse is as negative as it is today, is it not time to rethink the stereotypes of progressive historical change and the wonderful will of the people?

Of course, this is *not* an argument against trying to change the world. However, just as a counselor or therapist needs to understand her patient or client before seeking change in them, the left needs to realistically look at how human beings act and what they tend to believe. This means sometime, perhaps a great deal of the time, the left will be a minority and unpopular. But it beats going around claiming the people somehow are great. They just get fooled every time. It is really opportunism parallel to those who run for election and praise the people since they need their votes. Even our scientific experts have moved into deeply probing anew human aggression and propensity to divide the world into *us* and *them* (see the wonderful book by Robert Sapolsky, 2018). It is hard to read the new science of humans without surrendering some of the human-centric nature of the Progressive-Hegelian heritage.

This is not to exaggerate the sad state of the world either. The work of Pinker (2011) is an empirical analysis of how violence, in all its forms, has actually *declined* over many centuries. The issue is not that the world is going to hell in a handbasket but that people are very lazy and resistant to change and, often, do not share the beliefs of the left.

(2) *The myth of a benevolent state.* The ironclad belief in, and obsession with, the state as a center of progress has also been disproved. I am always somewhat amazed at how state-centric progressives and (not a few, even more) radical people are. Haven't they ever been harassed by a police officer or frightened by sirens of police following their cars? Have they never been audited or even threatened with an audit by the IRS? Have they been an immigrant trying to enter America? Or have they even just been on a long motor-vehicle bureau line?

Unfortunately, Marx and Engels erred, in a major way, in thinking the state would, even for a time, serve as a vehicle of liberation for people. In retrospect, it seems amazing even now that at a time when the states of Europe were dominated by monarchy, nobility, and military, they could envision something different. Most social scientists of all stripes acknowledge that the state's major role (whether they approve or not) is that of social control of the population (police, jails and prisons, a monopoly on violence, taxing powers, etc.) and the military to preserve the borders of the land that the state claims. Of course, the state does other things, and some may be good. But these are not the sine qua non of a state. The state arose initially to almost everywhere as a way to control the population and protect the power of the kings and emperors.

I have long been somewhat critical of libertarianism as a complete ideology given the state's role in social welfare and redistribution. These aspects such as providing social benefits to people and mildly progressive income taxes on the wealthy were hard-won benefits of previous struggles. Still, when I think about it, many private companies have competent bureaucracies as well: Amazon is great at getting products quickly to people's houses, for example. We have to separate what are technical problems (delivery of checks and medical care, for example) and what are intrinsic benefits of a nation-state. Here, while complete libertarianism may not work, the other extreme is perhaps far worse. For decades, the progressives and many on the broader left have told those who would listen to them to go ask the state in one way or other. The approach of pleading to government officials, who almost always are allied with the upper classes and concerned with their own fundraising, often fails. As I have suggested, it is only when pleading turns to possible disorder or threat that, at some periods of time, such appeals work (e.g., the 1930s and 1960s). But is it worth it? For six decades, reformers have advised poor people to fight for more welfare benefits. In addition to this strategy being a lot like banging one's head against the wall, it reifies and supports repressive, controlling systems. Welfare—whether it is called Aid to Families with Dependent Children (AFDC), Temporary Assistance for Needy Families (TANF), General Assistance, or some other name—is pitiful in amount, embarrassing, and controlling of one's life. At least, proposals for a guaranteed income (unlikely to succeed) raise the question of a guarantee without stigma and dependence on the state (other than awaiting the checks). This proposal could bring libertarians together with leftists.

The left as it is needs to be able to answer where in the past or present has there existed a fair state—one which is not allied with elites and which is not committed in the bulk of its resources to military and internal public control. I have not received a good answer to this because of the American left's naivete. Years ago, some people believed that the Soviet Union and China had achieved this utopian state, but with a little research into these states, they would see how sadly things turned out. Recently in the more moderate times on the left, Scandinavian nations have been a favorite citation of the left; but in my experience, most people who talk about them know little about these nations. Distance seems to promote admiration. Of course, some of these states have more social welfare programs, but that does not make those they have fair or admired by the folks who need to apply for them. While the military budgets, of course, are lower in small nations, all of them are capable of violently controlling their people. Sweden, for example, has shown little hesitancy in firing at protesting crowds in several years of international meetings there. The Swedish state has always had a cozy relationship with large capital there and so has the labor movement. All the nations support America and have sent troops to wherever our leaders demand—for example, Iraq and Afghanistan. One can say that aspects of states and societies represent some compromises between periods of unrest and radicalism, which leaves a residue of reform; and this can be said of Sweden, which at one point had a very radical working-class movement and still has, probably, among the higher percentages of workers organized in unions.

But such manners of speaking, which may be of interest to academics, do not work on the streets or in a punchy political message! Should you tell protesters in Sweden to take it easy on their state because it's better than some others? This would be a rather bizarre strategy and would, no doubt, be mirrored by conservatives, moderates, and liberals in the USA, saying it's better here than in most other countries. The situation in societies can certainly be altered by protests and revolutions. But to put all one's faith in a new state among a sea of strong capitalist nation-states is an error, and many radical movements from Nicaragua to Venezuela to Greece have erred in putting their faith in the state. And the possibility of a left (usually lacking any universal level of support by far) taking over a state and transforming it is not an idea that has historical support. Only several years ago, we have the illusion of the radical group Syriza winning election in Greece, claiming it could succeed in getting Greece out of the claws of the EU and IMF and potential bankruptcy. As Panagiotis Sotiris puts it, Syriza's "dream ... became a nightmare" (in Principe and Sunkara 2016) with its failure and then complete rejection at the polls.

(3) *While self-righteousness can be found throughout the spectrum of opinion, the Left's ugly embrace of "political correctness" has alienated many people*

As I write this in October 2019, a wonderful moment in the political culture occurred when Ellen DeGeneres (the prominent gay comedienne and, according to the media, a liberal) was spotted by the media at a football game enjoying a joke with former president George W. Bush. This may or may not be news, but the reaction of so many people who clogged DeGeneres's social media accounts with attacks and criticism was news. I received several Facebook posts myself from acquaintances criticizing DeGeneres for the incident, citing Bush as a war criminal. Wow, America today is really something!

I am no fan of W. in the least, but the self-righteousness of the left never ceases to amaze me. First, if he is to be characterized as a war criminal, why more than all our other recent presidents (aside from possibly Ford and Carter) who led us into countless direct and proxy wars all over the world? Obama is responsible, for example, for many deaths in Yemen, Libya, Somalia, and Afghanistan, to name only a few places. But second, what does it help to be hostile constantly to those we disagree with? Maybe some angry people like this way of living and can isolate themselves from people whose political and social views disturb them. Unfortunately, the political correctness–self-righteousness gambit exhibits a left (if one calls it that) with no power but to rant and criticize and show superiority over others.

I warned many years ago (Wagner 1997)[13] that political correctness had a strong class component in which middle-class educated people could criticize and feel superior to many lower- and working-class people who did not appropriately name a minority group or who did not express the current "correct" view of an issue. In fact, political correctness began as a leftist in-joke in the 1970s in response to the Chinese line expressed often on the left that one had to be "correct" in speech and action to align with Mao's thought (see Ellis 2002 for his history of politically correct thought, one I experienced coming from radical circles at Columbia University in the late 1960s). Who would have dreamed, as a young '60s leftist, that people would be spending their times correcting the general public on such issues rather than fighting for change? Edward Luce puts this well by pointing out that the critics often did not adhere to the appropriate beliefs themselves. So, when Barack Obama and Hillary Clinton criticized those who were not for gay marriage, they did not mention that neither of them were for it either before 2013 (Luce 2017, p. 186). Actually, go back a decade before, and few Democrats were for gay rights at all. But Luce also makes an even more important point:

"Second, the moral tone almost always boomerangs. People feel patronized ... Presumably they are on the wrong side of history, which is not a place anybody wants to be ... suggesting they are moral outcasts if they fail to see it." (ibid.)

Many on the left seem to have never learned the basic art of communication, much less the introductory course on community organizing. People do not change their minds by being hectored and lectured to or, even less, by being embarrassed or made to feel inferior. When I was a labor organizer, I found instinctively that difference and discrimination could be overcome only when people work together. I directly observed how white workers speaking in prejudiced ways *could* move past that when working on actions and getting to know nonwhite workers over time. They had their own aha moments, not fed to them by their bosses or academics or outside experts. Of course, this is not always true, but it is apparent in every study that people who get to know the other personally—whether racial and ethnic groups or people of different sexual orientations or of religions or genders—and begin to share some collective endeavor can overcome prejudice. Often it begins with a worker saying, "Oh, John, well, I don't think of him as

blank (fill in African-American, Jewish, Asian, gay, etc.),"
which sounds funny because the person wants to exclude a
person he knows as being different like a model minority.
But if the connection with the one coworker or acquain-
tance can be broadened, somehow change can be made. In
a micro sense, this is what happened in the United States
with gay rights as more and more people came out and
people began either to know people or were relatives of
people who were gay, lesbian, bisexual, or transgendered
and began to see popular figures (like DeGeneres) who
were gay.

Polls suggest what people view as political correctness
to be extremely unpopular (for example, see polls by Edsall
2015 and more recently by Blaze 2018; also see Stephen
2019 on the exhausted majority). It is probably one of
the strongest things Republicans and, perhaps, moderate
Democrats have against the idea of a progressive liberal
running for office. But ironically, political correctness,
because of its ties to identity politics (see below), fits nicely
into the move in capitalism toward segmented markets. In
the older days of modernist capitalism, appeals were made
to a broad majority—whether the mass media, advertising,
or political campaigning. In the recent decades, advertising
and mass media have become more adept at appeals not
only by age, region, gender, race and ethnicity, and sexual

orientation but also by hundreds of special interest groups from gun owners to wrestling fans to cooking enthusiasts. It has become more common to have targeted audiences and targeted appeals. The left too has abandoned what had been a unitary appeal to the large masses of people in the nineteenth to the mid-twentieth century, which were the working class, and joined the segmented market, appealing now and again to women, to gays and other sexual minorities, or to immigrants from different nations. The problem is that unlike marketing, the left's idea of liberation is very different from selling products. Once the left begins to exclude large groups of people—whether it is white men or people from the red states—it really loses more than a statistical number, and it loses its legitimacy as claiming to be for a change that would help all people. I think many sectors of the population feel that the new social movement of the left does not include them.

(4) *Reform masquerading as radicalism.* The so-called new social movements such as feminism and environmentalism were reformist; and their ideas for change, while important and much spoken about, are often vague. Identity politics—developed from the women's, African-American, and the gay-lesbian-bisexual-transgender movements (GLBT)—are like selfies of the movement. They

have become arenas of self-praise and sometimes dislike for others.

I remember quite well when many of what sociologists refer to as the new social movements arose (they do so to separate the older movements such as labor, socialism, or civil rights, for example, from the new movements of the late 1960s and afterward). Several of the movements, particularly the women's movement and the gay movement, grew out of the broader left movement. Research on the literature of both the history of the 1960s left as well as these movements supports that the initial cadre were often women who were radicalized by the civil rights and anti-war movement and who resented how they were treated by groups like Students for a Democratic Society (SDS) (for example, see Sayres et. al. 1984). Similarly, being at Columbia University in the late 1960s, I remember a number of gay men around the left, many of whom had not yet "come out." When the Stonewall rebellion occurred in 1969, radical gays (and some lesbians and some bisexuals) joined the protests in Greenwich Village and began to form their own groups in New York City. Although the move toward nationalism in the African-American movement began earlier (by a few years), around 1968–1969, groups such as the Young Lords (a primarily Puerto Rican organization that organized itself as a kind of twin of the

Black Panthers for Chicanos and other Hispanics) and the American Indian Movement (AIM) formed in 1968. The environmental movement was somewhat different as Earth Day started in 1970, a rather moderate affair developed by Senator Gaylord Nelson of Wisconsin. It took several years for the movement to have a noticeable left face to it.

None of these movements initially saw themselves as replacing a broader left. Frequently, chants by the Panthers and Lords, for example, would include references to "black, brown, white, or yellow"; and their references to "smashing the state" or capitalism were not meant to form a state of people of color, of women, of gay people, or of any specific group. However, unlike the conditions in nations like Western Europe where a strong left existed at the time, what had been the student and anti-war movement began to collapse, and there was little unitary or dominant organization or faction on the left. In many countries, women's organizations, environmental groups, and ethnic minority groups were associated with the broader left parties, but not in the USA after the early 1970s. This meant that fairly soon after they formed, the new social movements moved to being solely reformist organizations. There were always women, and I know a few to this day, who have a more radical or socialist vision of feminism, but they were small in number. And the arena to challenge equal pay, sexual harassment, the fight for the ERA (Equal Rights Amendment) or abortion rights, etc. seemed to be more fruitful at the governmental level and in alliance with those liberals who supported these particular issues. This similarly came to be the fate of all the other movements. In the absence of much of an organized left, those who seemed to hold power to help people of color, gays, and lesbians and to meet environmental demands seemed to be liberals. Again, this was not universally true in the 1970s, when people from these groups or members of leftist groups became defensive sometimes about this strategy. But soon enough, demands that liberation be total, for all, began to fade with the 1960s; and even arguments that ending sexism would benefit men and ending homophobia would benefit all began to drift when pride in being some identity took center stage.

A thought experiment on reformism is worthwhile. If I say I want to overthrow capitalism, my goal is fairly clear. If you went out for a vacation and the capitalist state and system were overthrown (as in, say, Soviet Union or China), you would notice the difference pretty soon. A great example is the film *Good Bye, Lenin! (2003)* in which a family struggles to hide the overturning of communism while an ill parent had been disabled, and the fun was in how hard it was. But what constitutes a revolution or total victory for the other groups? What would make us wake up and say, "Oh, things are totally different"? It is not easy to say. Women's rights have achieved admirable victories since the late 1960s in the United States and in most of the world. But most who remain feminists, I think, are not completely happy with this, as there remains much yet to be done. While I agree, what is a measure of total victory? In the early pre-identity days, such as MLK speaking of a nation where race does not matter, is that a goal of the women's movement—a society where gender does not matter? I tend to doubt it. Can exact equality with men be achieved, and perhaps more importantly, can it be sustained? And can it be sustained without lowering conditions of men (for example, in wages) rather than lift women up? There isn't quite an answer. This is the same problem for sexual minorities or people of color. Should groups be represented proportionately, which, in some cases, are not very large numbers? Should they be overrepresented, like some leftist groups have done, to overcome past injustice? There is no easy answer. Environmentalism, though of course a movement that is different, raises the same questions. Usually environmentalists attack a specific issue: oil spill, global warming, nuclear energy, or specific degradations of the environment. But none of these portends an absolute victory. In fact, in all the example, only radicals who incorporate a socialist or anarchist or ecofeminist or eco-radical position can do so. But then they are falling back more to a leftist perspective, and they are a small minority of people who support such efforts. For most women, LGBT, or ethnic minority groups, there is no end in mind, no utopia, which means there is also sometimes little recognition of progress.

In the 1970s, when there were still remnants of a left, those of us who were radicals, at least among my friends, were pretty aware that these were reformist movements, without much of a real radical center. However, of course, this was not a popular view among strong adherents of the new identity movements. The problem is that in casting aside a left, the movements became part of the Democratic Party machine and, in some cases, became so narrow as to alienate others. It is hard to pin down the origin of *identity politics* as a term, but it certainly, by recent decades, began to be a fitting description of many of (the nonradical) vocal proponents of the movements reliant on an identity (e.g., sex and gender, color, and ethnicity). I see the change from radical to reform movements to identity movements as, of course, a continuum; but there are disturbing elements to the change. Whereas in earlier days of the movements, usually those who were not *of* the identity itself had their support, more and more (depending on the group) men become unwelcome in a group for women's rights, whites

(and presumably other people not black) are not encour-
aged to be in African-American groups, and so on. There
is not always a sign on the door to meetings now in these
post–civil rights days ("No Men, No Whites"); but groups
can, if not prohibited, be made to feel very uncomfortable.
I have been in groups where support is accepted but not
any criticism. I talk as one who, for many decades, did not
feel this. Perhaps because of my politics and involvement
with some of these movements, I never felt excluded and,
except for minor corrections (your term there is *sexist* and
the like), felt little discomfort. Over the years—and I don't
think I am just more sensitive—I have experienced some
surprise at those who judge that I can't understand because
I am a man, white, not gay or lesbian, and so on. That
brings us to the point where we have gone from reform to
exclusion to, in some cases, hostility. In the olden days of
the 1960s, 1970s, and maybe into the 1980s, someone who
got up and condemned all men, all whites, and all straight
people were often disagreed with and sometimes corrected.
This is no longer true, perhaps because the others who
might disagree have left these groups. After all, activism in
any movement—whether women's, gay, environmental, or
socialist—is voluntary. It is, in fact, often against interest
in being long hours of meetings or demonstrations or plan-

ning. If a group does not support you, you need not come back, and you need not be active at all.

Of course, the mass media and political system enjoy these splits in potential movements immensely. The media declares movements where no sociologist would see one, such as the so-called Me Too movement, which was totally media invented. They love the word *movement* though they use it incorrectly in a sociological sense. The media and the Democratic Party are both well set up for identity groups. They are a beat in the newspapers and TV; they are predictable. They are caucuses in the Democratic Party and must be contended with. We are now in a nation where some people believe they can find out all about a person by looking at them and observing their apparent sex, race, age, and so on. From these crude measures, people think they can determine who may be an ally or not. This is, of course, not a new state of affairs to those discriminated against; but it is not advance, but a retreat.

Finally, perhaps the worst news is that as identity politics becomes what most people think of as the left, the liberatory project of the left of the period between the mid-nineteenth century and the early twenty-first century declines. I have not met a person who is working-class or poor who believes all women, including Oprah Winfrey or Meryl Streep or Hillary Clinton, are oppressed or that all African-Americans—including James Earl Jones, Ben Carson, or Steve Harvey—are oppressed as well. The vague and non-sociological view that someone may be affected by racism on the street by a hostile passerby or may be more prone to attack by a husband or partner does not make these acts oppression, which is a term reserved for state and elite powers. If oppression is anything, it is state sponsored or assisted systematic actions against a group of people. It trivializes the concept to think of affluent minorities as oppressed. After all, rich people are subject, in many places, to more property crime than others, as they look rich and have fancy cars and nice houses. In places where there are many people of color, it is not a rarity for a white person to get called honky or cracker when an argument breaks out. None of this is reason to discuss oppression. But it is a case to say that identity politics, as a vague source of anger, has gone too far and eventually leads to a backlash effect.

(5) *Being all over the place.* The left (and the right as well) seems to have an opinion on everything and anything. Rather, the left should concentrate on a few clear goals and basis of unity. While perhaps true of all ideologies, the left feels compelled to discuss the daily weather to assess its relevance for climate change, violent crimes that take place on a daily basis particularly if they include identity victims, and wide range of other issues that they may know little

about. Unfortunately, this tendency runs into many dangers: it may alienate people who otherwise agree with some of left thinking (but not others), it may be wrong because ill-informed, and worst, it may lead to a kind of totalitarianism in which each breath of society is analyzed for its faults, some of which may be human nature.

There seem to be many (and all) issues parts of the left, at least, criticize and comment on. Among many, immigration and climate change are two of the biggest newer issues. For most of the left history, there was no position on immigration though, of course, refugees who are leaving nations because of political or other differences were always supported. But there was no unity or clarity on the left whether America should have two million or two thousand immigrants. The recent change, of course, is partly caused by the worldwide surge of poor immigrants from many countries in the Middle East especially, but also Africa and Eastern Europe (the collapse of Yugoslavia, for example). Anyone with a conscience should be concerned about what has happened in the last decades and how so many people can be kept alive in their travels and accommodated safely and without prejudice. And indeed, the concern crosses political lines. It is, after all, German prime minister Angela Merkel who has shown some leadership in her nation and the European community in accommodating immigrants despite the fact that her party is a conservative one. Yet because of Donald Trump's well-known anti-immigrant bias and prejudiced statements, for nearly three years of his presidency, every action taken on immigrants—whether efforts at baring certain immigrants or the conditions of the deportation camps—has brought loud cries of protest from the anti-Trumpers. Few seem to remember it was only a number of years ago that "advocacy groups criticized then-President Obama as the 'deporter in chief'" (CNN 2019). The data on deportations is complicated in part because of changing definitions, but according to the Migration Policy Institute, the Clinton administration deported twelve million people; the Bush administration, ten million; and Obama, five million. As CNN reports, Trump's, despite his rhetoric, deportations are lower, though there are also fewer people attempting to come in perhaps because of Trump's blustering threats (ibid.). The complex tit-for-tat political debate is not one with a clear end. If the left supports open borders, which no nation in the world has, it is unlikely to succeed with public opinion, much less get Congress's support. Perhaps realizing this and, as always, supporting the Democratic Party, no one seems to mention this as a proposal. In other words, no one mentions the unmentionable that all people should be let in. What I am suggesting is, while we can favor a humanitarian approach to immigration and, perhaps, policies that are more generous for immigrants who are fleeing oppression and political refugees (think of the thousands of Jews on ships turned away by the United States during the 1940s and the many thousands of Haitians denied immigrant status despite fleeing a dictatorial regime), we need not open borders entirely. This does not mean every action of any administration is necessarily evil nor does it mean ICE should be (or will ever be) abolished. Unless we have an anti-state movement in general, it is silly to raise the call as an isolated issue (e.g., why not abolish IRS, Homeland Security, and all the other social control agencies?).

Climate change has become a grand issue of much of progressives and those further left. One important question here is, What expertise does the left bring to the scientific table? In my experience, not very much. I remember the days when scientist Paul Ehrlich (*The Population Bomb*) predicted that worldwide famine would occur in the 1970s and 1980s because of overpopulation. This finding was widely embraced by the left and frequently mentioned at meetings and in conversations. Fortunately, the predictions turned out to be untrue, but the apocalyptic warnings were embraced. Similarly, I can remember the panic of the nuclear reactor's going off-line in 1979 at Three Mile Island. I actually know of a leftish group that left their New

York City homes to flee to Florida to avoid the possibility of fallout. As I discussed (in 1997, footnote 115, p. 196), responses to the AIDS crisis were also apocalyptic. As if the crisis was not enough, the left had to predict hundreds of millions would die, and they missed the point that Africa would be the locus of death (see Stephen Jay Gould, a left-leaning scientist who predicted "AIDS would dwarf the Black plague" and kill off one-quarter of the world's people) (ibid.).

If the left were an erudite group of scientists, it would be one thing, but generally people just parrot those views that seem to reflect theirs. As Eduardo Porter pointed out in the *New York Times* (2016), the left is not pro-science any more than the right. It opposes science in nuclear energy despite a Pew Poll showing most American scientists actually support it. Countries like Sweden and France with large social democratic parties have invested far more than the US in this area. Further, the left stands against genetically modified organisms (GMOs) although, again so far, no scientific evidence supports that they are unhealthy. I am not necessarily suggesting the left even reverse its biases. It seems more in order to hold off pronouncements on issues that do not reflect any expertise of its members.

The embrace of the apocalyptic disaster is not a pretty picture of the left (and the religious right as well). It seems too easy for those who hope for monumental changes to perhaps believe the end is near because of capitalism or because of corruption or blindness of leaders. Yet as we see, new experiments in Iceland are actually finding that carbon dioxide can be taken from the air and converted to rocks (Richard 2019). Although this interesting breakthrough seems too expensive to be a method worldwide, there is a chance that science (as it did with overpopulation) can overcome the climate change issue. One wonders if good news would be acceptable to the left (or the right, which is busy denying the problem). How committed are radicals to apocalyptic endings or at least to only apocalyptic endings?

The reach all over by the left seems frenetic and desperate. It digests headlines as if everything is fodder for propaganda, and maybe it is. But thoughtfulness is sometimes left out at a desire to counter the right or the current administration or some other enemy. It seems to me, as I will suggest below, that the left has had a lot more historic experience with some things more than others; and to crowd a hundred issues onto the plate does not necessarily play to what could be a stronger, if simpler, left.

How Progressivism Has Made Problems Worse in Recent Decades

Although, as I have argued, the problems with the left are multicausal and many have their roots in classic Marxist and Leninist thinking, there is little question that in terms of criticisms one and two, these problems have worsened in recent years as the left sheds its connection with Marxism or anarchism to turn to progressive reformism.

While I have noted that Rousseau's concepts of the masses as always correct started a couple centuries of overly optimistic thought, the ideology of Marxism and other left-wing groups, such as anarchism and syndicalism, rejected the notion that running for office or getting appointed to a government post had anything to do with the type of change they supported. Although, of course, many thinkers argue back and forth about the classics, the key statements of Marxist-Leninism are that the state was a creature of capitalism and that the only way the state could change would be by, as Lenin said in *The State and Revolution*, the state being crushed by a revolution of the proletariat.[14] Concretely, this meant that all aspects of the state—the military and security apparatus, its bureaucracy, its political representatives, and its agencies—needed to be totally replaced and totally reorganized by revolutionary people.

So, while leftists may have been too optimistic about the coming of revolution, they certainly did not believe electing someone to a bourgeois political office would have any effect on capitalism. It was the fundamental break between communism and social democracy after World War I that separated those who were revolutionaries and those who believed a slow gradual process of reform would somehow change capitalism. It is amazing that nearly a century after this break, today's progressives seem satisfied to vote for one or the other candidates with the idea that this will somehow change the system in America (the position that the social democrats had).

Nowhere historically can progressives find that social democrats led significant change in the twentieth century. The social democratic and other reform parties in France, United Kingdom (Labor Party), Germany, Italy, and dozens of other nations around the world led to zero significant change in their countries. Even the brief periods where leaders adhering to social democracy stood in an alliance with Communist parties, they hardly made a revolution as the leadership of Léon Blum in the 1930s and François Mitterrand in the 1980s did in France shows and the failure of Allende in Chile as well. After a century of experiments by social democrats and progressives, the verdict is in. Clearly, except for raising of some social benefits, no major changes in capitalist power have occurred in any nation through the electoral process (Brazil's leftist hero Lula provides another example of the progressive left changing few things in this large nation after seven years).

In the sense, the overly optimistic progressives also have dropped any critical notion of the state to believe our political system is wide open to any changes, including socialism. The incredible naivete even of a seasoned sociologist like Richard Flacks is amazing:

> "That Bernie Sanders could win a vast popular following while calling himself and his program 'socialist' really challenges the way SDSers thought about the matter. It seems that the newest Left is emerging with a clearly stated aim of going beyond capitalism—and that 'socialism' provides a label for that. "(Flacks and Flacks 2018, p. 366)

As Flacks admits after the above, in fact, Sanders's program is *not* socialist but a collection of reforms, not going beyond the limits of liberalism and progressivism. To say one is for universal health care is to ally oneself with most of the world, hardly a socialist proposal, particularly in the absence of riding the US of its private, for-profit health-care industry. Raising taxes on some richer people and corporations is not socialist, nor are proposals for free tuition at some schools or a bailout plan for college debt. All these reforms are supported by Elizabeth Warren, who has said she is a capitalist (https://www.dailywire.com/news/elizabeth-warren-i-am-capitalist-come-i-believe-hank-berrien). To present socialism as a campaign that is well within the capitalist framework is to mislead people and, probably, to lead people to disillusion. A victory (unlikely) for either Sanders or Warren, as we have discussed, is unlikely to achieve its stated goals, much less change the US government and capitalism in any significant way.

Another thing we have learned from decades of international political posturing is to take the label *socialist* with a grain of salt. There was a time when socialism was a needed label to attract working-class voters, and so national socialism under fascism and Christian socialism in much of the world never had to do with achieving socialism. This led to dozens of countries around the world changing their parties to the name "socialist." Africa in the 1960s and 1970s had dozens of nations subscribing to African socialism. Other Third World countries also had similar parties. These labels of socialism again had little to do with any desire to achieve socialism, but they were useful in tweaking the American and European imperialists, helped warm up relations with the Soviet Union and China, and evidentially, pleased voters in these nations for a while. So simply because a candidate or even a party makes some noises about socialism, it does not mean any real commitment to socialism.

Things Can Change Quickly Sometimes

Although the politics and ideology of a time sometimes seem immutable, change actually occurs and sometimes quickly. Who would have thought a few years ago of Donald Trump leading the Republicans in office or liberal progressives regaining their power in the Democratic Party? It is true that perhaps with progressives, it will take a major victory even nationally or perhaps in a number of states for the dead-end quality of their reform efforts to be seen. A winner, as noted in the Brooks article about Warren, would have little chance nationally and even in most states to affect the ambitious rhetoric that many progressives use. This could lay bare what progressives can actually do and whether they stand for anything other than centrist democratism.

It would not require a huge number of people to bring together a new party, which was sharply opposed to using the Democratic Party as a vehicle and insisted on independent organizing and an emphasis of engaging grassroots people, particularly the non–middle class of the nation in an organizing recruitment drive. Obviously, it would have to arise from a lowly position as funders are not necessarily friendly and the media coverage of the two parties are hardly guaranteed to any other party. If such a party is to be successful and bring forward new ideas and experiences for an American left, it would have to identify with a socialist past, albeit critically and constructively moving to a new understanding of what democracy may mean, neither clinging to the past nor to nice-sounding clichés that overrate the ability of the average person to tolerate endless meetings. People want to fight on certain issues but do not want to enter a church or a council of governance as much as the new ecological radicals or anarchists believe. [15]In addition to anti-capitalism, a new party has to identify authoritarianism as an enemy in any form; as we know, governments use nice rhetoric to oppress and that public and nonprofit sectors also have a large role in hierarchy as much as business and corporations. As has been its history, war and violence should be its enemy. We cannot believe in just wars or terrorism and other action that is sometimes justified for whatever reason.

As noted, the many issues spoken of by progressives, perhaps in the hundreds, perhaps can be left for other

groups to lead. Though commanding little of the population, the left acts as if it needs a caucus of every group,
race, ethnicity, and sexual affiliation. Much of this is really
an opportunistic tactic by the left as much as mainstream
centrist and other groups. The fact is, a political party or
group will never, in this identity age, represent a subgroup
of the population nor should it.

To be successful, a new party would have to go back
to the old idea that the Socialist Party under Debs once
had: that elections were a place to get visibility and to pros-
elytize. Unfortunately, even in their history, many people
became confused and thought they were campaigning to
win. But unless or until people in the United States have
some real idea of what a socialist society may look like, it is
futile to preach that elections will make for great changes.

REFERENCES

Appiah, K. "Class Act." *The New York Times Magazine.* September 2, 2018, p. 9.

Aronowitz, S. *The Death and Rebirth of American Radicalism.* New York: Routledge, 1996.

Becker, W. *Goodbye Lenin.* 2003 (film).

Berg, J. C. *Teamsters and Turtles? US Progressive Political Movements in the 21st Century.* Lanham, MD: Rowman and Littlefield, 2003.

Berry, M. *History Teaches Us: How Progressive Movements Have Succeeded in Challenging Times.* Boston: Beacon Press, 2018.

Black, R. http://the2020progressive.com/difference-liberal-progressive/.

Blaze. "Poll: Vast Majority of Americans Believes Political Correctness to Be a National Problem." October 12, 2018. https://www.theblaze.com/news/2018/10/12/poll-vast-majority-of-americans-believe-political-correctness-to-be-a-major-national-problem.

Bookchin, M. *Towards an Ecological Society*. Montreal: Black Rose Books, 1980.

———. *The Next Revolution: Popular Assemblies and the Promise of Direct Democracy*. London: Verso, 2015.

Boyer, R. and Morais. *Labor's Untold Story*. United Electrical Workers, 1975.

Brands, H. W. *The Strange Death of American Liberalism*. New Haven: Yale University Press, 2001.

Breuning, L. G. *How I Escaped Political Correctness and You Can Too*. Inner Mammal Institute, 2018.

Brooks, D. "A Brief History of the Warren Presidency." *The New York Times*. September 19, 2019.

Bynum, C. *A. Philip Randolph and the Struggle for Human Rights*. Springfield, IL: University of Illinois, 2010.

Campaign for Free College Tuition. "Support for Free College Is Strong." June 2019.

Center for Responsive Politics. "Top Individual Contributors: All Federal Contributors." OpenSecrets.com. 2019.

Chace, J. *1912: Wilson, Roosevelt, Taft and Debs—the Election that Changed the Country*. New York: Simon and Shuster, 2004.

Clymer, A. "A Liberal by Any Other Name May Get More Votes." *The New York Times*, Late Edition (East Coast). November 24, 1985: A.5.

Cohen, Robert. "Joseph P. Lash." American National Biography Online. 2000.

Cottrell, R. C. *Roger Nash Baldwin and the American Civil Liberties Union.* New York: Columbia University Press, 2000.

Court, E. and C. Feinstein. "From Donald Trump to Bernie Sanders, Here's How Much Every 2020 Presidential Candidate Has Gotten from the Healthcare Industry." *Business Insider.* August 5, 2019.

Croteau, D. *Politics and the Class Divide: Working People and the Middle Class Left.* Philadelphia: Temple University Press, 1995.

Culver, J. C. and J. Hyde. *American Dreamer: A Life of Henry A. Wallace.* New York: Norton, 2001.

Daily Wire. July 25, 2018. https://www.dailywire.com/news/elizabeth-warren-i-am-capitalist-come-i-believe-hank-berrien.

Dao, J. "Nader Runs Again, This Time with Feeling." *The New York Times,* Late Edition (East Coast). April 15, 2000: A.1.

Dickinson, T. "How a New Generation of Progressive Activists Is Leading the Trump Resistance." *Rolling Stone.* August 24, 2017.

"Difference Between Progressive and Liberal." Posted by administration on July 23, 2012. Accessed December 6, 2018. www.difference.between.com.

Dionne, E. J. "The Democrats in Atlanta, Dukakis Asserts Control." *The New York Times.* July 18, 1988: A.1.

———. "Jackson Share of Votes by Whites Triples in '88." *The New York Times.* June 13, 1988: B.7.

Doherty, E. "Many Americans Think Economic Inequality Is a Problem—Just Not the Most Pressing One." *538.* August 16, 2019 (2020 Election). https://fivethirtyeight.com/contributors/erin-doherty/

Dowd, M. "Jackson Is Arming His Campaign with Substance." *The New York Times.* April 7, 1988: D.22.

Dubofsky, M. *We Shall Be All: The History of the Industrial Workers of the World.* Champaign, IL: University of Illinois Press, 2000 (orig. 1969).

Douthat, R. "All the President's Privileges." *The New York Times* (op-ed), Late Edition (East Coast). June 24, 2012: SR.13.

Edsall, T. "Alexandra Ocasio-Cortez Is Leading and Following at the Same Time." *The New York Times.* January 23, 2019.

———. "Trump, Obama, and the Assault on Political Correctness." *The New York Times.* December 23, 2015.

Ellis, F. "Political Correctness and the Ideological Struggle: From Lenin and Mao to Marcuse and Foucault." *The Journal of Social, Political, and Economic Studies*. vol. 27, issue 4, (Winter 2002): 409–444.

Ember, S. "Young Voters Still 'Feel the Bern,' but Not Just for Bernie Sanders Anymore." *The New York Times*. September 20, 2019.

Fawcett, E. *Liberalism: The Life of an Idea*. Princeton: Princeton University Press, 2018.

Flacks, M. and R. Flacks. *Making History, Making Blintzes*. New Brunswick, NJ: Rutgers University Press, 2018.

Flacks, R. *Making History: The American Left and the American Mind*. New York: Columbia University Press, 1988.

Flegenheimer, M. "Some Liberals Worry Clinton Faces Risks in Focus on Trump." *The New York Times* (national desk), Late Edition (East Coast). August 15, 2016: A.1.

Gibson, R. and P. Singh. *The Battle Over Health Care*. Lanham, MD: Rowman-Littlefield, 2012.

Gillespie, D. *Politics at the Periphery*. Columbia, SC: University of Southern Carolina, 1993.

Gitlin, T. "The Left Declares Its Independence." *The New York Times* (op-ed), Late Edition (East Coast). October 9, 2011: SR.4.

Goodman, J. D. and W. Newman. "Bill De Blasio Is a Progressive but Is He Progressive Enough?" *The New York Times*. July 26, 2018.

Green, D. *Shaping Political Consciousness: The Language of Politics in America from McKinley to Reagan*. Ithaca: Cornell University Press, 1988.

Green, M. *Bright, Infinite Future*. New York: St. Martin's Press, 2016.

Gregory, D. *Defining Moments in Black History*. New York: Harper Collins, 2018.

Gregory, R. *Norman Thomas: The Great Dissenter*. New York: Algora Publishers, 2008.

Hardy, K. "Nader, the Greens, and Building a Movement." *Dissident Voice*. March 7, 2008.

Hays, C. "Fair or Not?" *The New York Times*, Late Edition (East Coast). May 19, 1996:3.

Healey, D. and M. Isserman. *California Red: A Life in the American Communist Party*. Urbana, IL: University of Illinois Press, 1993.

Herbers, J. "Radicals of the '60s, Now Progressives. Recall Past and Plan for Futures." *The New York Times*. July 17, 1978: A.12.

Herndon, A. W. "2020 Democrats Agree: They're Very, Very Sorry." *The New York Times*. February 3, 2019.

———. "Working Families Party Endorses Elizabeth Warren. Here's Why It Matters." *The New York Times*. September 16, 2019.

Hofstadter, R. *The Progressive Movement 1900–1915*. Englewood Cliffs, NJ: Prentice-Hall, 1963.

———. *The Age of Reform*. New York: Vintage, 1960.

Holtzmann, A. *The Townsend Movement: A Political Study*. New York: Octagon Books, 1975.

Howe, I. *Socialism in America*. New York: First Harvest, HBJ, 1985.

Howe, I. and L. Coser. <u>*The American Communist Party*</u>. New York: Praeger, 1962.

Ifill, G. "Campaign: Democrats, Centrist Council Exults in Success of a Member." *The New York Times*. May 3, 1992: A.28.

Jacobs, M. *Demographic Delusions: Review of Ruy Teixeira the Optimistic Leftist. Dissent* (Winter 2018): 123–25.

Jakoubek, R. *Jesse Jackson: Civil Rights Leader and Politician*. Philadelphia: Chelsea House, 2005.

Klehr, H. *The Heyday of American Communism: The Depression Decade*. New York: Basic Books, 1984.

Knight, L. *Jane Addams: Spirit in Action*. New York: W. W. Norton, 2010.

Kolko, G. *The Triumph of Conservatism*. Chicago: Quadrangle Books, 1963.

Krugman, P. "Saints and Profits." *The New York Times* (op-ed), Late Edition (East Coast). July 23, 2000: 4.15.

———. "Loans and Leadership." *The New York Times* (op-ed), Late Edition (East Coast). March 28, 2008: A.23.

———. "The Obama Agenda." *The New York Times* (op-ed), Late Edition (East Coast). New York, June 30, 2008: A.19.

Landler, M. "Protests Offer Obama Opportunity to Gain, and Room for Pitfalls." *The New York Times*. October 7, 2011: A.13.

Laslett, J. J. and S. M. Lipset. *Failure of a Dream? Essays in the History of American Socialism.* Berkeley: University of California Press, 1984.

Lenin, V. I. *The State and Revolution: the Marxist Teaching on the State and the Tasks of the Proletariat in the Revolution.* Introduction by Norman E. Saul. Norwalk, CT: Easton Press, 1992.

Levin, J. and F. Silbar (eds.). *You Say You Want a Revolution: SDS, PL and Adventures in Building a Worker-Student Alliance.* San Francisco: 1741 Press, 2018.

Levin, M. R. *Rediscovering Americanism and the Tyranny of Progressivism.* New York: Simon and Schuster, 2017.

Lilla, M. *The Once and Future Liberal: After Identity Politics.* New York: Harper, 2017.

Lind, M. "Trumpism and Clintonism Are the Future." *The New York Times* (op-ed), Late Edition (East Coast). April 17, 2016: SR.2.

Luce, E. *The Retreat of Western Liberalism.* New York: Grove Press, 2018.

Macdonald, D. *Discriminations: Essays and Afterthoughts 1938–1974.* Grossman Publishers, 1974.

Mackay, K. C. *The Progressive Movement of 1924.* New York: Octagon Books, 1947.

Madigan, C. M. and M. Tackett. "How Jackson Built Leverage Time-Tested Strategy Paid Off, Series: A Change of Heart: The Jackson Candidacy." *Chicago Tribune.* August 7, 1988: 1.

Mahler, H. and Y. Alcindor. "Fixated on Campaign Fight, Sanders Risks Lasting Legacy." *The New York Times* (national desk), Late Edition (East Coast). May 23, 2016: A.1.

Mala, E. "Voices from the Front." *The New York Times.* January 19, 2012.

Manjoo, F. "Barack Obama's Biggest Mistake." *The New York Times.* September 18, 2019.

Marx, K. *The 18ᵗʰ Brumaire of Louis Napoleon.* London: Pluto Press, 2002.

Mascaro, L. "Trump's Election Has Mobilized a Resistance Like No Other, but Will Democrats' Answer to the

Tea Party Divide the Ranks?" *Los Angeles Times.* April 23, 2017.

McCormack, W. "Are You Progressive?" *The New Republic.* April 20, 2018.

Mitchell, J. "The Identity-Politics Death Grip." *City Journal.* (Autumn 2017).

Mulloy, D. J. *Enemies of the State: The Radical Right in America from FDR to Trump.* Lanham, MD: Rowman-Littlefield Company, 2018.

National Park Service. "Andrew Jackson's Speech to Congress on Indian Removal."

December 6, 1830. http://www.nps.gov/museum/tmc/MANZ/handouts/Andrew Jackson Annual Message.pdf.

NPR. "As More Democrats Embrace 'Progressive' Label, It May Not Mean What It Used to." October 29, 2018.

Nugent, W. *Progressivism: A Very Short History.* New York: Oxford University Press, 2009.

"On the Issues: Ralph Nader." https://www.ontheissues.org/Ralph Nader.htm.

Oreskes, M. "Jackson Nudging Democrats to Left." *The New York Times*, Late Edition. April 24, 1988: A.24.

Orwell, G. *Homage to Catalonia.* New York: Harcourt, Brace and World, 1952.

Ottanelli, F. *The Communist Party of the United States.* New Brunswick, New Jersey: Rutgers University Press, 1991.

PBS. *The Great Depression.* Episode 5, "Mean Things Happenin' in the Land." 1993.

Pfeffer, Paula. "Asa Philip Randolph." In *American National Biography Online.* 2000.

Pinker, S. *Better Angels of Our Nature: Why Violence Has Declined.* New York: Viking Press, 2011.

Pitts, L. "Change, Resentment, and the Hate in the Air." *Chicago Tribune.* March 13, 2017: 17.

Piven, F. F. and R. Cloward. *Poor People's Movements: Why They Succeed, How They Fall.* New York: Pantheon, 1977.

————. *Regulating the Poor: The Functions of Public Welfare.* New York: Vintage, 1993 (orig. 1971).

Porter, E. "Climate Change Bias, but on Both Sides." *The New York Times.* April 20, 2016: B.1.

Príncipe, C. and B. Sunkara (eds.). *Europe in Revolt: Mapping the New European Left.* Haymarket Press, 2016.

Progressive Party Platform 1924. https://left.wikia.org/wiki/Progressive_Party_Platform,_1924.

Rappeport, A. "Democrats Tangle in New Hampshire Over Rights to 'Progressive' Label." *The New York Times* (national desk), Late Edition (East Coast). February 4, 2016: A.14.

———. "Democrats' Plan to Tax Wealth Would Reshape US Economy." *The New York Times*. October 1, 2019.

Ratcliffe, R. "Jackson Cites Need for Unity; Dukakis Gets Praise but No Endorsement." *Houston Chronicle.* July 20, 1988: 1.

Reich, R. "Democrats Need a New Strategy: From the Left." *Daily Press*. Newport News, VA, January 25, 2017: A.20

Reston, J. "Cuomo's Prescription for Democratic Victory." *The New York Times* (interview), Late Edition. February 9, 1984: B.12.

Richard, J. "Iceland Turns Carbon Dioxide to Rock for Cleaner Air." https://phys.org/news/2019-05-iceland-carbon-dioxide-cleaner-air.html.

Rosenthal, A. "Taking Cue from Reaganites, Liberals Are Drafting Blueprints." *The New York Times*. July 6, 1988: A.14.

———. "On My Mind; No Victory through Surrender." *The New York Times*, Late Edition. April 22, 1988: A.39.

Sapolsky, R. M. *Behave: The Biology of Humans at Our Best and Worst*. New York: Penguin Books, 2018.

Sayres, S., Stephanson, A., Aronowitz, S., and Jameson, F., (eds.). *The Sixties without Apology*. Minneapolis, University of Minnesota, 1984.

Scher, B. "How Liberals Win," *The New York Times* (op-ed), Late Edition (East Coast). July 1, 2012: SR.8.

Schmalz, J. "Cuomo's Years: The Words versus the Deeds." *The New York Times*. January 6, 1988.

Schmitt, M. "Is the Sanders Agenda Out of Date?" *The New York Times* (commentary), Late Edition (East Coast). June 16, 2016: A.23.

Schwartz, Howard S. *Political Correctness and the Destruction of Social Order: Chronicling the Rise of the Pristine Self*. Cham: Springer International Publishing (Palgrave Macmillan, imprint), 2016.

Sennett, R. and J. Cobb. *The Hidden Injuries of Class*. New York: Vintage, 1973.

Shaw, D. "Hedge-Fund Billionaires Were Democrats' Main Bankrollers in 2018." *The American Prospect*. May 16, 2019.

Stephens, B. "Howard Schultz Derangement Syndrome." *The New York Times*. February 1, 2019.

Suderman, P. "New Poll: Medicare for All Is Popular Until You Explain How It Works." *Reason*. January 24, 2019. https://reason.com/2019/01/24/new-poll-shows-medicare-for-all-is-popular.

Sumner, G. *Dwight McDonald and the Politics Circle: The Challenge of Cosmopolitan Democracy.* Ithaca, NY: Cornell University Press, 1996.

Swanson, M. *The War State: The Cold War Origins of the Military Industrial Complex.* CreateSpace Independent Publishing, 2013.

Taibbi, M. *Griftopia.* New York: Speigel and Grau Trade Paperbacks, 2011.

The New York Times (editorial). "What Jesse Jackson Has Won." April 21, 1988: A.30.

Toner, R. "Obama's Test: Can a Liberal Be a Unifier?" *The New York Times* (national desk), Late Edition (East Coast). March 25, 2008: A.1.

Unger, N. C. *Fighting Bob La Follette: The Righteous Reformer.* Chapel Hill, University of North Carolina, 2000.

Urofsky, M. *Louis D. Brandeis: A Life.* New York: Pantheon Books, 2009.

Verhovek, S. H. "Unlike '96, Nader Runs Hard in '00." *The New York Times,* Late Edition (East Coast). July 1, 2000: A.8.

Wagner, D. *The New Temperance: The American Obsession with Sin and Vice.* Boulder: Co., Westview-Perseus, 1997.

————. *The Quest for a Radical Profession: Social Service Careers and Political Ideology*. Lanham, MD: University Press of America, 1990.

————. "Radical Social Movements in the Social Services: A Theoretical Framework." *Social Service Review* 63, no. 2 (1989): 264–84.

Weaver, W., Jr. "Democrats' Platform Shows a Shift from Liberal Positions of 1976 and 1980." *The New York Times*, Late Edition (East Coast). July 22, 1984: A.20.

Weiner, G. "When Liberals Become Progressives, Much Lost." *The New York Times*. April 13, 2018.

Weinstein, J. *Ambiguous Legacy: The Left in American Politics*. New Viewpoints, 1975.

Wiebe, R. *The Search for Order, 1877–1920*. New York: Hill and Wang, 1967.

Wikipedia. https://en.wikipedia.org/wiki/Jesse_Jackson.

Wolf, Z. B. "Yes, Obama Deported More People than Trump but Context Is Everything." CNN Politics. July 13, 2019.

Zeballos-Roig, J. "A New Poll Found the Aggressive Medicare for All Plan Bernie Sanders Has Championed Is Getting Less Popular as Time Goes On." *Business Insider*. October 15, 2019.

INDEX

A

Addams, J, 16, 47, 66-68, 69, 70, 72, 77

Affordable Care Act (ACA), 31, 172, 182

AFL-CIO, 66, 121, 128

African-Americans, 44, 46, 49, 67, 72, 102, 107, 112, 127, 128, 130, 131, 133, 141, 143, 167, 170, 188, 219, 220, 221, 225, 227-28, 258n., 259n.

Allende, S., 204, 235

Alsop, J., 117

American Civil Liberties Union (ACLU), 116, 152

American Indian Movement, 222

American magazine, 51

American Railway Union (ARU), 53

Americans for Democratic Action (ADA), 117

Anarchism, 40, 47, 54, 68, 75, 98, 105-6, 109, 110, 116, 118, 122, 129, 130, 131, 133, 170, 228

Anderson, J. B., 80

Anti-war movement, 164, 201

Arafat, Y., 141

Argentina, 205, 207

Aronowitz, S., 13–14

B

Babbitt, B., 136

Baldwin, R., 98, 105-6, 109, 110, 116, 118, 122

Bentsen, L., 151

Berger, V., 54

Berry, M., 108

Bezos, J., 199

Biden, J., 166, 176, 187, 191, 193, 194, 199, 201

Bismarck, O., 43

Black Muslims, 131

Black Power, 131

Blair, T., 136

Bloomberg, M., 199

Blum, L., 235

Bonus March, 73, 83

Brandeis, L., 16, 66, 73, 86

Brands, H. W., 128, 133

Brazil, 205, 206, 210, 236

Bread and Roses Strike, 54

Brexit, 210

Bridges, H., 88

Brotherhood of Sleeping Car Porters (BSCP), 107

Browder, E., 91,103, 113-115

Brown, R.,94

Bryan, W. J., 80

Bull Moose Party. See Progressive Party
of 1912

Bush, G. H., 40, 134, 152, 159

Bush, G. W., 40,134, 152, 169, 171, 172, 174, 216, 230

Businessweek, 113

busing,132, 136

C

Cambodia, 204, 259n

Capitalism, 7, 13, 16, 29, 30, 37-38, 49, 56, 76, 82, 101,
104, 110, 113-14, 115, 118, 119, 127, 142, 157, 158,
159, 160, 186, 206, 209, 215, 219, 222,223, 233,
234, 235, 236, 237, 239

Carter, J., 134, 135, 157, 216

Castro, F., 141

Chaplin, C., 119

Child labor reform, 17, 61, 90

Chile, 204, 205, 207, 235

Chiles, L., 136

China, 30,121, 133,204, 205, 207. 235

Churchill, W., 115

City manager system, 59, 61

Civil Rights Act, 46,75,129

Civil rights movement, 18, 42, 69, 75, 108, 129, 130, 139, 141, 155, 221, 226

Clinton, H., 25, 29-30, 166, 167-170, 175–181, 217, 227

Cold War, 40, 82, 115, 128

Comintern (Soviet Union), 57, 257n

Communist Party USA, 7, 15,17, 18-19, 27-29, 32, 34, 81-125, 135, 201

Communist Political Association, 114

Comte, A., 20

Congress of Industrial Organizations (CIO), 97-98

Conservatives, 11-12, 14, 17, 18-19, 23, 37-45, 58, 83, 94, 115, 126, 128, 134, 135, 138, 148, 151, 157, 178, 196, 215, 230

Coolidge, C., 17, 70

Cottrell, R. C., 98, 106

Crime bill (1994), 136, 155

Croly, H., 2, 16, 65, 66

Croteau, D., 130

Curran, J., 116

D

Daughters of the American Revolution (DAR), 69, 94

Davis, J. W., 17, 71

Dean, H., 134, 180

Death penalty, 137,155, 258n

De Gaulle, C., 204

DeGeneres, E., 216, 219

Democratic Leadership Council (DLC), 136

Democratic Party, 9, 11, 13-14, 15-16, 17, 18, 19, 26, 27, 28, 29-30, 33, 34, 35, 40, 46, 48, 49, 67, 85, 91, 117, 119, 124, 125, 127, 129, 133, 134, 136, 139, 140-1, 146-150, 152, 161, 165-195, 200, 201, 202, 225, 227, 230, 238

Democratic Socialists of America (DSA), 206

Dewey, J., 72

Dewey, T., 120, 258n.

Dimitroff, G., 92

Disraeli, B., 43

Dixiecrats, 46,49

Dos Passos, J., 95

Dreiser, T., 96

Du Bois, W. E. B.,72

Duclos, J., 114

E

Earth Day, 222
Edsall, T., 19, 219
Edwards, J., 134
Ehrlich, P., 231
Einstein, A., 119
Eisenhower, D., 128. 167, 258n.
Environmentalism, 21, 22 38-9, 49, 75, 132, 133, 163, 175, 220, 222, 223, 224, 226, 258-9n.
Equal Rights Amendment (ERA), 145, 223
Eychaner, F., 199

F

Fair Labor Standards Act, 62, 89, 90
Fascism,92, 93, 98 102, 124, 237
Fawcett, E.,127
Federal Trade Commission (FTC), 62
Feminism, 15, 22, 62, 77, 222, 224, 257n.
Flynn, E. G., 16
Ford, G., 46, 145, 216
Foster, W. Z., 116
France, 93, 202, 204, 232, 235
Franco, G., 96
Frank, W., 95

Front organizations (of Communist Party), 82, 95, 98, 105, 106, 109, 122

G

Galbraith, J. K., 117
Garfield, J., 96, 119
Gay marriage, 176
Genetically modified organisms (GMOs), 232
Gephardt, D., 136
Ghetto riots (1960s), 75, 131
Goldman, E., 105
Goldwater, B., 128, 258n
Gompers, S., 66, 72
Goodman, A., 209
Gore, A., 25, 134, 136,142, 150, 153, 162, 167,
Gorsuch, N., 185
Gould, S. J., 232
Grand Alliance, 18, 82, 111
Great Depression, 42, 53, 73, 75, 85, 86, 87, 89, 101, 194, 208
Greece, 93, 207, 215
Green, D., 82-83
Green, M., 9-10, 139
Green Party, 14, 140, 153, 161-63
Guaranteed annual income, 43, 76, 133, 148, 213

H

Harding, W., 70

Harris, F., 134

Harris, K., 9, 191, 199, 213

Hayden, T., 139

Haymarket Riot, 50

Hegel, G. / Hegelianism, 20, 208, 211

Hellman, L., 96

Hepburn, K., 119

Hill, J., 54

Hitler-Stalin Pact, 17, 28, 82, 107, 109-110

Hoffman, R., 199

Homophobia, 223

Hoover, H., 83, 86

Horton, W., 152

House Un-American Activities Committee (HUAC), 116,
    121

Howe, I., 103-4

Howe, I. & Coser, L., 84, 104, 112, 114, 116, 121, 124

Hudson, R., 99

Hughes, L., 96

Humphrey, H., 117, 129

I

Iceland, 233

Identity politics, 33, 46, 155, 177, 178, 188, 219, 220-1, 223, 225, 227-8, 240

Immigration issues, 24, 41, 42, 45, 49, 53, 59, 67, 186, 215, 228-230

Industrial Workers of the World (Wobblies), 16, 34

Iraqi War, 40, 167, 170, 214

J

Jackson, A., 21, 118

Jackson, J., 123, 127, 134, 140, 141-152,153, 155, 160, 164

Jakoubek, R., 151

Japanese-American internment camps, 67, 112

Jews/Jewish, 53. 102.142, 231

Jim Crow laws, 49, 112, 128

Johnson, H.,69,

Johnson, L. B., 127, 128

K

Kavanaugh, B., 185

Keller, H., 72, 109, 119

Kelley, F., 72

Kemp, J., 138

Kennedy, E., 134

Kennedy, J., 126, 128, 185

Kerry, J., 25, 134

King, M. L., 131

Koch, E., 150

Kolko, G., 16, 52, 56, 63, 64

Krugman, P., 142, 169, 174

Ku Klux Klan (KKK), 71

L

Labor Party (British), 235

Labor unions, 16, 17, 41, 54, 59, 62, 65, 66, 72, 75, 90, 99, 100, 103, 107, 113, 117, 121, 122, 128, 155, 214

La Follette, R., 16, 17, 37, 39, 47, 59, 60, 66, 67, 68, 69, 70-1, 72, 74, 76-77, 83, 123, 184

Laissez-faire, 16,49, 71, 136

Lamar, H., 119-20

Landon, A., 91, 258n.

Lash, J., 106, 108-9

Lawrence, MA, 54

League Against War and Fascism (later the League for Peace and Freedom), 98, 105

League of American Writers, 110

Lenin, V. I., 121, 122, 223, 234

Levin, M., 11-12, 32

Lewis, A., 138

Lewis, J. L., 97

Liberals/liberalism, 11-12, 13, 15, 16, 17, 23, 24, 26, 27, 30, 31, 32, 33, 36, 37-46, 51, 66, 78, 81, 83, 84, 85, 88, 92, 94, 98, 104, 117, 119, 120, 126, 127, 128, 129, 133, 134, 136, 137, 138, 139, 140, 141, 142, 145, 146, 152, 153, 155, 162, 163, 165, 167, 169, 171, 178, 181, 182, 187, 190, 192, 195, 199, 201, 203, 219, 223

Libertarianism, 32, 44, 212, 213

Lilla, M., 165, 187

Lippman, W., 16

London, M., 54

Long, H. Share the Wealth program, 87

Los Angeles, 26, 81

Los Angeles Times, 114, 189

Ludlow, CO, 55

Lula (de Silva), 236

Lundeen Bill, 89

M

MacArthur, D., 86, 106

Macdonald, D., 95

Mackay, K. C., 17

Magda, 101

Mahler & Alcindor, 177, 180- 181

Mao Tse Tsung thought, 122. 217

March on Washington Movement (MOWM), 108

Marijuana legalization, 44, 136, 146, 155

Marshall Plan, 119

Marx, K., 20, 85, 114, 121, 122, 208, 211, 234, 260n

Mascaro, 189. 191

McAdoo, W., 71

McCain, J., 158, 170

McCarthy, J., 115

McCarthy, M., 95

McCarthy period, 29, 82, 100, 121

McClure's magazine, 51

McGovern, G., 72, 132, 134

Medicare, 75, 179, 192 193

Merkel, A., 229

Mesabi Range, 55

Migration Policy Institute, 230

Minimum wage, 42, 43, 90, 154, 182

Mitchell, H., 87

Mitterrand, F., 235

Mondale, W., 134

Moore, M., 154

Moscow Trials, 95-6, 106

Muckrakers, 16, 48, 51-52

Mugwumps, 52

Murray, B., 154

Muste, A. J., 34, 86

N

The Nation, 96, 124

National Association for the Advancement of Colored
    People (NAACP), 67

National Journal, 169

National Negro Congress, 106, 110

National Public Radio (NPR), 11

Native Americans, 21, 49, 82, 143

Nazi Germany, 91, 96, 109, 111, 208

Nelson, G., 222

New Deal, 1, 8, 27, 34, 42, 62, 78, 81, 83, 84, 88, 89,
    111168

New Left, 33, 46, 122, 129, 131, 204

The New Republic, 96, 124

New Right, 44, 46, 127,134, 148

New social movements, 13, 203, 220, 221, 222

New York City, 18, 23, 24, 54,108, 130, 142, 150, 170, 221

The New York Times, 12, 23-24, 126, 135, 138, 139, 142, 148, 149-50, 171, 173, 177-78, 180, 187, 192, 232

Niebuhr, R., 110. 117

Norris, F., 52

Norris-LaGuardia Act, 73

North American Free Trade Agreement (NAFTA), 154, 185

No-strike pledge (World War II), 113

Nuclear energy, 224, 231, 232

Nunn, S., 136

O

Obama, B., 25, 26, 40, 158, 160, 166, 167-74, 176, 177, 179, 183, 184, 187, 188, 189, 190, 201, 210, 216, 217, 230

Ocasio-Cortez, A., 29, 30

Occupy Wall Street, 19, 35, 164, 170-1, 177

Operation Breadbasket, 141

Operation Desert, 152.

Orwell, G., 99

Ottanelli, F., 96, 99, 102-3, 111, 113

P

Palmer Raids, 70

Parker, D., 96

Partisan Review, 95

Paterson, NJ, 54

Pelosi, N., 186

People United to Save Humanity (PUSH), 141

Perkins, G. W., 56

Personal Responsibility Act (1996), 137

Pew Poll, 232

Pinker, S., 211

Piven, F. F. and Cloward, R.,8

Political correctness,13, 33, 203, 215–20

Pollitt, K., 155

Pol Pot, 205, 259n

Poor People's Movement, 85

Popular Front, 7, 16, 17, 19, 82-84, 91-126, 166, 195, 196, 201, 257n

Populism, 77, 136, 192

Porter, E., 232

POUM, 97

Powell, A. C., 103

Progressive Party of 1912, 16-17, 67, 77, 79

Progressive Party of 1924, 8, 70-74, 79, 82, 102, 115

Progressive Party of 1948, 18,79, 82, 102, 115-122

first Progressive movement (1900s–1920s), 12, 16, 35, 47, 55

second Progressive movement ('30s, '40s), 18, 70

Prohibition, 71

Protective legislation, 61

Public Interest Research Group (PIRG), 112

Public works programs, 38, 89

Pullman Strike, 50

Pure Food and Drug Act, 17, 52, 62

Putin, V., 206

Q

Quill, M., 117

R

Rainbow Coalition, 143, 144

Randolph, A. P., 107-08

Recall, referendum, and initiative, 61

Regulatory reforms, 62

Rendell, S., 140

Reparations for slavery, 46, 145, 146, 147

Republican Party, 10, 14, 17, 40, 44, 47, 48, 49, 50, 56, 59, 91. 93.120, 127, 128, 129, 133, 134, 172, 173, 185, 191, 195, 198, 199, 200, 219, 238

Reuther, W., 117

Robbins, T., 154

Robinson, E. G., 119

Rockefeller, J. D., 55

Rolling Stone (magazine), 190

Romney, M., 173

Roosevelt, E., 109, 117

Roosevelt, F. D., 19, 42–43, 46, 49– 50, 61

Rousseau, J. J., 207

Russian Revolution, 22, 101

S

Sapolsky, R., 211

Sarandon, S., 154

Schlesinger, A., 117

Schmitt, M., 117

Schumer, C., 151-3

Scientific Management (Taylorism), 66

Seattle anti-globalization protests, 34, 163-4

Segregation, 49, 108, 112, 128, 132

Sennett & Cobb, 130

Sexism, 135, 223, 226

Sherman Antitrust Act, 67

Simon, P., 134

Simons, J. H., 199

Sinclair, U., 16, 17, 51, 52-3

Sit-down strikes, 91

Slagle, B., 149-150

Smith, A. E., 71

Smith Act, 111

Snowden, E., 169

Social democrats, 11, 92, 161, 167 179, 204, 205, 206,208,232, 23592

Social fascists, 92

Socialism, 13, 29, 30, 32, 33, 36, 37-46, 71-72, 76, 79, 85, 92, 97, 102, 113, 161, 177, 179, 184, 201, 204, 206, 208, 221, 222, 224, 226, 236-8

Socialist Party, 8, 16, 17, 34, 53-4, 55-56, 71-72, 73, 86, 87, 91, 92, 107, 108, 123, 240

Socialist Workers Party, 111

Social justice, 23, 156

Social Security Act, 9, 18, 24, 25, 26, 34, 38, 42, 75-76, 88, 89, 133

Sorel, G., 54

Soros, G., 198

Sotiris, P., 215

Southern Tenant Farmers Union (STFU), 87

Soviet Union, 17, 30, 72, 82, 87, 95, 96, 100, 101, 102, 106, 109-110, 111, 115, 117, 119, 136, 145, 204, 205, 206, 208, 214, 223, 238

Spanish Civil War, 96

Stalin, J., 17, 28, 82, 92, 94, 96, 101, 107, 108-110, 115, 121, 122, 195, 204, 205, 208, 258n., 259n.

The State and Revolution (Lenin), 234

Steyer, T., 199

Stone, R., 138

Stonewall rebellion, 221

Students for a Democratic Society (SDS), 34, 221

Sussman, D., 199

Sweden, 30, 214, 215

Syndicalism, 54, 234

Syriza Party, 215

T

Taft, W. H., 55, 64

Taft-Hartley Act, 116, 120

Taibbi, M., 173

Tarbell, I., 16, 51-52

Temperance movement, 50, 259n

Tenney, J., 27

Thatcher, M., 205

Third Way, 136

Thomas, N., 91, 93

Three Mile Island nuclear accident, 231-2

Townsend movement, 34, 77, 86, 88, 89

Trail of Tears, 21

Treaty of Versailles, 73

Trotskyists, 87, 95, 97, 111

Truman, H., 108, 117, 118, 120, 127, 128

U

Udall, M., 134

Unemployed Councils, 34, 86

Unger, N., 59-60, 72, 76-77

United Kingdom, 35, 92, 136

Universal health insurance, 36, 145, 147, 154, 200

University of Wisconsin, 69

V

Vietnam War, 34, 40, 129, 133

Voting Rights Act, 25, 145, 205

W

Wagner Act (National Labor Relations Act), 34, 89

Wald, L., 16

Wallace, H., 18, 79, 82, 84,102, 118, 119, 120, 122, 153, 162, 184

War on drugs, 44, 144

Weaver, W., Jr., 135

Weissman, R., 197-98

Welfare reform. See Personal Responsibility Act (1996)

Welfare rights movement, 43

Welfare state, 42, 43, 88

White, W. A., 57

Wilentz, S., 12

Williams, H., 110

Women's suffrage movement, 45, 67

Workmen's (now workers') compensation, 62, 63

World Trade Organization (WTO), 34, 163

World War 39, 54, 67, 38, 207, 235

World War II,73, 82, 108, 111-15, 207

Y

Yorty, S., 27

Young Lords Party, 221

ENDNOTES

1 Although I do not. See chapter 3.
2 To take only one example of an issue I will return to, the Communist Party and its allies were one of the main forces in the social work left (see Wagner 1989, 1990) exemplified in New York by the Radical Alliance of Social Service Workers. While they dominated leadership and committee work, the more radical members of the group demurred the very liberal (or progressive) politics of the group for a more Marxist, radical, openly socialist, or socialist-feminist ideology. The CPers used to the Popular Front wanted all activism devoted to within the Democratic Party and/or the professional association, the National Association of Social Workers, while radicals called for independent action.
3 Co-optation was a wonderful word used extensively in the late 1960s. Efforts to absorb protest and protesters and their supporters are rather constant in America (except where violence and other suppression occur). Usually there is a carrot of reform and the stick of repression, and usually both are employed. As an example, in the 1930s, the government and enlightened businessmen absorbed unionists into the system, while radical strikes were repressed and outlawed by labor law.
4 People today, including some scholars, appear to be uncomfortable with the word *line*. For example, Ottanelli's history of the Communist Party (1991) agrees with almost all the facts about the CP but strains—and seems to be the main purpose of his book—to present the party as an indigenous movement that was its own guide. But his argument is weak as he admits the Soviet Union and

the Comintern made unilateral changes in the party line. He just notes, and I do not disagree, that some of the changes may have been inevitable, but that is not much of an argument.

5   They still are and, to my knowledge, have never taken full responsibility for their support of Stalinism.

6   I well understand that in America, people do not want to associate with communism. However, unless the left as a group of organizations, magazines and newspapers, and leaders do hold open discussions on how to proceed, they continue a top-down manner of organizing. As I discuss in chapter 6, the left continues to suffer from rigidity and righteousness and has not learned from past mistakes.

7   The Republican Party nominees for president against FDR all came from its liberal wing—Alfred Landon, Wendell Willkie, and Thomas Dewey. Eisenhower, while best described as a moderate, considered running as a Democrat in 1948, and he was close to the Eastern Establishment of the party. Only in 1964—with Barry Goldwater's nomination and later, of course, Ronald Reagan— was the GOP more clearly a party of the right. Republicans also had many elected officials and voters who were more isolationist than cold warriors.

8   Discussions of King tend to leave out how much militant African-Americans attacked him in the two or three years before his death. To followers of Malcolm X, SNCC (Student Nonviolent Coordinating Committee), the Black Panthers, and many average African-Americans, King appeared as a sellout in those heated days.

9   Of course, some issues are affected more than others; and anything with a touch of racial injustice—such as crime, death penalty, or welfare—is highly affected. However, American attitudes toward protest groups of all sorts, including environmental or women's groups, were also affected. Many Americans saw large crowds of people who looked like hippies or dissenters negatively, and for some, the constant complaining led to a compassion fatigue on many issues. Others had a kind of guilt-by-association view as

most of these groups—women's movement, gay and lesbian movement, and environmental movement—came out of the left.

[10] Of course, I do not mean to imply these questions are easy. But there have been many experiments in workers' control over enterprises from Russian Soviets to Yugoslav factory control, having consumers or stockholders of sorts control under Tito to "co-determination" in Germany and some other European nations. Having consumers or stockholders of sorts control enterprises has also been debated in Europe, and whether poorly executed or not is part of the framework of socialist nations as the public through its government is meant to control the enterprises.

[11] The left has always been underdeveloped in the United States, and there are many theories why. I grew up with the New Left, which made an incredible amount of noise but did not seek deep roots into most of America.

[12] The left, in fact, has been extremely dishonest on some issues of nationalism, racism, and discrimination. When African-Americans of nationalist beliefs (Louis Farrakhan, for example) spread hatred of whites and Jews, the left is reluctant to criticize them. Leftists often seize on people as heroes and are extremely late (if at all) with realizing their ills, whether it was Pol Pot in Cambodia, Robert Mugabe in Zimbabwe, or Idi Amin in Uganda, for example. Their belief in heroic Asian and African oppressed people blinded them to the dictators. The left's support for a boycott of Israel—whose government I, too, detest—makes me uneasy because the Israeli regime is still no worse than all the other Middle East nations, which should all be boycotted. One could ask women or gays, for example, if they would rather live in Israel or Saudi Arabia, Syria, Egypt, or Iran. It is a no-brainer.

[13] I must admit no one commented on this aspect of the book although the term had been in wide use since the 1980s. I described the moralizing of politically correct politics as being similar to middle-class movements about drugs and alcohol and tobacco, sexual behavior it did not like, fatty foods, and other temperance movements.

[14] Most Marxists believe Marx himself had a similar view of the state, perhaps best explained in his book *The Eigteenth Brumaire of Louis Napoleon* (Pluto Press 2002). His partner Friedrich Engels did, in his later years, form a comfortable relationship with the German socialists and others who had begun to take a more reformist position.

[15] Unfortunately, the left, such as anarchist and municipal socialist Murray Bookchin (1980, 2015), engages in considerable wishful thinking. Learning from the oppressive Stalinist regimes, many on-paper reformers pledge a kind of low-level democracy in which everyone would run everything. Unfortunately, anyone with any experience not only in politics but also in society knows that, first, the least favorite thing of many people is to attend endless meetings and that, second, those attracted to this life are usually those of higher class. Take any city, even a small one, and count up the hundreds of boards of public, nonprofit, and private organizations. You total many thousands of people, almost all of whom have a vested interest in the system and are affluent.

ABOUT THE AUTHORS

David Wagner is an emeritus professor of sociology and social work at the university of Southern Maine and the author of twelve books including the award-winning *Checkerboard Square* and *The New Temperance* as well as *What's Love got to do with it?*, *The Poorhouse,* and *Confronting Homelessness.*